Teaching Adults

Teaching Adults

A Handbook for Instructors

Gary Dickinson

new press
Toronto 1973

ISBN 0-88770-714-9

First printing

123456   78 77 76 75 74 73

new press

Order Department
553 Richmond Street West
Toronto, Ontario
M5V 1Y6

Design: Pamela Patrick
Typeset by Compose
Printed by Alger Press, Oshawa, Ontario
Manufactured in Canada

contents

introduction

Every year more than twenty million adults in North America participate in part-time and continuing education programmes offered by public-school systems, university extension departments, business and industrial firms, labour unions, agricultural extension services, voluntary organizations, and a host of other agencies. Most of the instructors in such courses are involved in adult education on a part-time basis. The instructors tend to have considerable expertise in their main occupation, but they usually lack even the most fundamental knowledge, skills, and attitudes necessary for teaching adults. As a result, a poor quality of instruction is often provided to adult learners so that many of them become dissatisfied with the learning experience and drop out. The enthusiasm and technical knowledge possessed by part-time instructors are highly desirable qualities, but a background of training in the principles and practices of teaching adults would enable them to create a much more satisfying and effective learning situation.

The best method of providing training in adult education for the large number of people who teach adults on a part-time basis is by direct contact with experts in that field and with other part-time instructors. Whenever such opportunities are made available, the response is usually overwhelming. Unfortunately, few part-time instructors have either the time or the opportunity to take a comprehensive training programme in adult learning and instruction. This book was written in an attempt to meet some of the learning needs of the part-time and beginning instructor.

Four basic criteria were kept in mind while the book was being written:

1. The general principles presented should be applicable in a wide range of adult instructional settings.

2. A systematic treatment of adult learning, course planning, and instruction would provide a consistent framework and point of view for the part-time instructor.

3. Current research and theory would be readily understood by instructors lacking a background of study in education if it were translated into practical terms.

4. Only material having direct usefulness to part-time instructors should be included so that the book would be relatively brief and concise.

The book is organized in five chapters headed Adult Learning, The Adult Learner, Course Planning, Instruction, and Evaluation. There are review frames interspersed throughout which could serve the reader as notes and as a summary of the material contained in that section. Each chapter is followed by a brief list of books that are recommended for further study. Most of these references are obtainable in paperback editions at relatively inexpensive prices. A brief test precedes and follows each chapter so that the reader can examine his own state of knowledge before and after he reads the material.

The principles, practices, and suggestions contained in the following pages were tried out and developed with hundreds of part-time instructors who attended short courses and workshops on teaching adults. They provided valuable assistance toward the development of the material contained in this book.

how to use this book

Each chapter is preceded and followed by a ten-item test. Before you begin a chapter you can determine your current state of knowledge by completing the pre-assessment. The score that you obtain will serve as a guide to reading and studying the material. When you finish a chapter, complete the post-assessment form to find out how well you have learned the material.

You are asked to make two responses to each item in the pre- and post-assessment forms. First, indicate whether you think the statement is true or false. Second, indicate the degree of confidence that you feel about the answer you gave. You may be 1) guessing, 2) think that your answer may be correct, or 3) confident that your answer is correct. When you have completed the assessment, score your response by referring to the correct answers on the page following the test.

Adjust your approach to each chapter depending upon the scores you receive on the pre-assessment. For example, if 9 or 10 answers are correct and the confidence level for each item is 2 or 3, just skim over the chapter. If you gave 7 or 8 correct responses and the confidence levels are scattered over 1, 2, and 3, read the chapter carefully. If 6 or fewer of your responses are correct and the confidence levels are 1 and 2, study the chapter carefully and mentally try to apply the material to your own teaching.

Complete and score the post-assessment when you have finished reading and studying the material in each chapter. If you have less than 8 items correct, re-read the chapter and try to obtain some of the suggested references in order to increase your knowledge in the areas where it is weak.

1

ADULT LEARNING: PRE-ASSESSMENT

Before reading chapter one, complete the pre-assessment test given below. Indicate whether each statement is true or false, and your degree of confidence in your answer.

Correctness of Statement   Degree of Confidence
T The statement is true.   1 I guessed at the answer.
F The statement is false.   2 My answer may be correct.
    3 I'm confident that my answer is correct.

1. Learning always results in a change in the learner's behaviour.   T F 1 2 3
2. The learning process is more effective in the formal instructional setting than in the natural societal setting.   T F 1 2 3
3. Changing the instructional technique will cause the learning rate to decline.   T F 1 2 3
4. Memorizing the multiplication tables is an example of learning in the psychomotor domain.   T F 1 2 3
5. Riding a bicycle is an example of learning in the cognitive domain.   T F 1 2 3
6. Developing interest in a subject is an example of learning in the affective domain.   T F 1 2 3
7. Learning that is reinforced is less likely to recur.   T F 1 2 3
8. Distributed practice is more effective than massed practice with inexperienced learners.   T F 1 2 3
9. Knowledge of results that is delayed for three days is a useful way of helping adults to learn.   T F 1 2 3
10. Reproducing past learning is referred to as recognition.   T F 1 2 3

Please turn to the next page for the correct answers and score your chapter one pre-assessment.

ANSWERS

1. T; 2. T; 3. F; 4. F; 5. F; 6. T; 7. F; 8. T; 9. F; 10. F

If you had 9 or 10 correct answers and confidence levels of 2 and 3, skim over chapter one. If you had 7 or 8 correct answers and confidence levels of 1, 2, and 3, read the chapter carefully. If you had 6 or less correct answers and confidence levels of 1 and 2, study the chapter in detail and think through the applications of the material to your own teaching.

adult learning

An understanding of how adults learn is essential to someone who is or intends to become a part-time instructor in an organization concerned with adult education or adult training. The ultimate goal in every activity of teaching adults is to help and encourage them to learn something that they didn't know before. Thus, there is a close relationship between the processes of learning and the activities of instructing. Instruction can't be designed and carried out effectively without an understanding of what is happening while an adult learns.

Learning is an *internal* process that varies from person to person, while instruction is *external* to the learner. The teacher of adults has no direct control over the internal process of learning, so there is no guarantee that the external acts of instruction will result in learning. Based on our understanding of how adults learn, however, it is possible to arrange external conditions in order to increase the probability that learning will occur.

> *From the viewpoint of the learner:*
> *1. Learning is an internal process.*
> *2. Instruction is an external activity.*

IDENTIFYING LEARNING

When used by psychologists, the term *learning* has a broader meaning than when the same word is used in everyday conversation. What is learned does not necessarily help the adult; something may be learned accidentally, or the learned material may be incorrect. Thus, we can and often do learn bad habits, incorrect patterns of speech, or faulty skills.

Those kinds of learning that are not particularly helpful to us are most likely to occur in situations known as the *natural societal setting*. Learning in that setting is a normal result of everyday living and may be accidental and unintended. It is also an inefficient way of learning which may even be harmful to the learner since no one is guiding the activity. Learning can be more efficient and useful in a *formal instructional setting* where it occurs under some direction. In this setting, the instructor controls the external conditions of learning by organizing material and presenting it in such a way that the desired changes have a better chance to occur than if the same material was learned by accident in the natural societal setting.

> *Learning occurs in:*
> 1. *Natural societal settings.*
> 2. *Formal instructional settings.*

The chief concern of the teacher of adults is with learning in the formal instructional setting. This is usually thought of as a classroom in a school, but it may also include other facilities such as a factory, store, office, community meeting hall, church, pub, private residence, or any other place where adults can gather for purposes of learning. Although the places where guided learning can occur are many and varied, the element common to all formal instructional settings is that someone is responsible for arranging the external conditions of learning to increase the probability that learning will occur.

In either the natural societal or the formal instructional setting, it is important to recognize whether or not learning is taking place. There is no widely accepted definition of learning to assist in its identification, but there are four elements common to all learning activities. If the following characteristics are present, then we know that some learning has occurred.

1. *Learning results in a change of behaviour.*
When an adult learns, he is able to do something that he couldn't do before, or he can do it better than before. If his observable behaviour does not change, then he has not learned.

2. *Learning occurs through practice.*
For simple activities only a few short practice sessions may

be needed. For complex learning activities such as reading or operating a typewriter, several years and thousands of practice sessions may be required.

3. *Learning produces a relatively permanent change.*
Things that are learned tend to last for a considerable period of time. A person who has learned to swim at ten years of age could probably still swim at age thirty even if he hadn't touched the water during the twenty-year interval. Temporary changes that occur while 'under the affluence of incohol' or because of fatigue are not considered to be learning.

4. *Learning is not directly observable.*
It is not possible to observe learning directly because very complex mental processes are involved. We can observe such activities as the instructor speaking and the learner writing notes, but those actions do not necessarily indicate that learning is taking place.

> *Learning:*
> 1. *Results in a change of behaviour.*
> 2. *Occurs through practice.*
> 3. *Produces a relatively permanent change.*
> 4. *Can't be directly observed.*

Two of the characteristics of learning noted above have special implications for the teacher of adults. The concept of learning as behavioural change serves as the basis for planning programmes of instruction and carrying them out successfully. Planning and teaching activities are most effective when done in terms of learner behaviours rather than instructor behaviours or the subject matter to be taught. In this way, the learner and his behaviour become the central focus while the instructor and the material are of secondary importance. The fact that learning is not directly observable introduces an element of uncertainty into the whole process of teaching adults. While the instructor does his best to create a situation in which learning can occur, there can be no guarantee that it will. This may result in feelings of insecurity and doubt on the part of the instructor, but in the element of uncertainty lies the challenge of teaching adults.

6

LEARNING RATES

Learning in the formal instructional setting occurs at different rates under different circumstances. Each new group of learners proceeds at a different rate, and there is a considerable variation among learners within a single group. An individual adult may display an inconsistent learning rate at different times and his rate of learning will vary with different kinds of material.

A useful way of illustrating how learning progresses over a period of time is by a *learning curve.* The curve in Figure 1 shows the rate of learning commonly found for simple material such as new words in a foreign language. Learning tends to occur rapidly at first, followed by a gradual levelling off as the material is mastered.

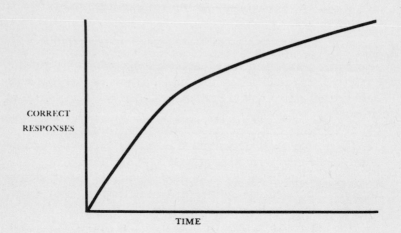

Figure 1. Learning Curve for Simple Material

The learning curve in Figure 2 illustrates a typical rate for learning complex material or skills such as typing. Learning proceeds slowly at first, then gradually accelerates, and finally levels off.

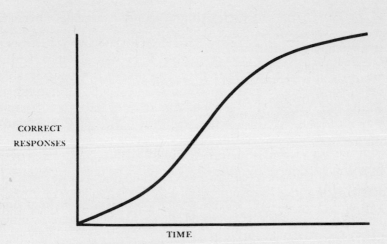

CORRECT
RESPONSES

TIME

Figure 2. Learning Curve for Complex Material

Learning curves generally have *plateaus*, which are periods of relative standstill where no new learning seems to occur. There are several possible explanations for the occurrence of plateaus:

1. The learner may be tired or suffering from fatigue.
2. There may be a decline in the learner's level of motivation, or he may have lost interest in the material.
3. The learner may have paused to think about simple material and arrange it in a different form so that a new stage of complex learning can begin.
4. No new learning may be occurring but incorrectly learned material is being eliminated.

The instructor should attempt to identify the relevant cause of each learning plateau so that appropriate action can be taken. If the plateau results from fatigue or loss of interest, the instructor could change the instructional technique, call for a short rest period, or switch to different material in order to send the learning curve upward again. If it is apparent that the learner is reorganizing previously learned material or eliminating incorrect material, then a review period, group discussion, or even five minutes of silence could be arranged by the instructor.

> *Two concepts that help to explain learning rates are:*
> 1. *Learning curves.*
> 2. *Learning plateaus.*

DOMAINS OF LEARNING

There are many different things that an adult can learn from participating in a learning activity in the formal instructional setting. As those things are learned in different ways and involve varying kinds of learner behaviours, the teacher of adults should be able to recognize the major kinds of learning and plan his guidance of the learning process accordingly.

The many behaviours that can be learned are classified into three broad areas or *domains of learning*. The *cognitive* domain emphasizes the learning of information, intellectual skills, and problem-solving behaviours. The *affective* domain is concerned with interests, attitudes, and values, while the *psychomotor* domain deals with motor skills such as machine operation or the use of tools. Although some learning activities are concerned primarily with a single domain, many involve two or even three domains at the same time. Learning to type, for example, is primarily psychomotor but the typing instructor may also attempt to convey information about the correct form of a business letter as well as to develop a professional attitude towards office work. When the chief concern of the instructor is with the cognitive domain, the students may be learning certain attitudes towards the instructor and the subject matter at the same time.

> *The domains of learning are:*
> 1. *Cognitive.*
> 2. *Affective.*
> 3. *Psychomotor.*

Within each domain of learning, learner behaviours can be arranged in a progressive sequence ranging from simple to complex. An adult will have greater ease in learning if new material in a specific domain is presented in the sequence suggested for that domain.

In the cognitive domain, the behaviours range from the simple recall of factual information to the complex practice of making critical judgements. The six categories of behaviour in the cognitive domain include:

1. *Knowing.* The learner needs only to remember bits of information, principles, and methods of dealing with problems.

2. *Comprehending.* The learner is able to understand a communication but does not necessarily relate it to other material.

3. *Applying.* The learner can apply abstractions or general principles to specific situations.

4. *Analysing.* The learner can break down a communication into its elements and see their inter-relationships.

5. *Synthesizing.* The learner can arrange and combine elements into a new and unique whole.

6. *Evaluating.* The learner can make judgements about the value of using materials and methods for specific purposes.

Learner behaviours in the cognitive domain:
1. *Knowing*
2. *Comprehending*
3. *Applying*
4. *Analysing*
5. *Synthesizing*
6. *Evaluating*

Learner behaviours in the affective domain are more difficult to arrange in sequence than are those in the cognitive domain. All behaviours in the affective domain have an emotional component concerned with likes and dislikes, attitudes, values, and beliefs. The five categories of learner behaviour in the affective domain are listed below.

1. *Receiving.* The learner is willing to receive or pay attention to certain behaviours.

2. *Responding.* The learner becomes actively interested in the desired behaviour.

3. *Valuing.* The learner develops a consistent attitude

towards a behaviour or object and believes that it has worth.

4. *Organizing.* The learner organizes several beliefs and values into a system by determining their inter-relationships and establishing priorities.

5. *Characterizing.* The learner behaves consistently over a period of time in accordance with his value system so that it forms a philosophy of life.

> *Learner behaviours in the affective domain:*
> 1. *Receiving*
> 2. *Responding*
> 3. *Valuing*
> 4. *Organizing*
> 5. *Characterizing*

At the present time it is not possible to present a widely accepted sequence of behaviours for the psychomotor domain. Most psychomotor learning, however, could be placed in one of the following four categories:

1. *Gross bodily movements.* The learner is able to move his limbs either separately or in combination with other parts of the body.

2. *Finely co-ordinated movements.* The learner moves parts of the body in a pattern co-ordinated by the eye or ear.

3. *Non-verbal communication.* The learner is able to communicate using facial expressions, gestures, and bodily movements.

4. *Speech behaviours.* The learner transmits speech which involves forming, producing, and projecting sound.

> *Learner behaviours in the psychomotor domain:*
> 1. *Gross bodily movements*
> 2. *Finely co-ordinated movements*
> 3. *Non-verbal communication*
> 4. *Speech behaviours*

PRINCIPLES OF LEARNING

When he is designing learning activities for adults, the instructor should recognize that each person will learn at a different rate and that the type of material will influence learning. Although vast differences exist among individuals, certain basic principles are common to all adult learning. An understanding and application of those principles will help the instructor to select and use instructional processes that will provide the best learning opportunity to the adult student for each type of material presented.

Meaningful Material

Material that the learner believes to be meaningful is learned more readily and is remembered longer than material which is seen as non-meaningful. *Meaningfulness* can be established in two general ways: by presenting material that is similar to something that is already known, and by organizing new material in a pattern that the learner can perceive.

The instructor's perception of what constitutes meaningful material often differs from the learner's perception because of differences in their previous experience and training. In many cases, the vocabulary of terms used by the instructor may be entirely unfamiliar to the learner, and this may block the learning process. Meaningfulness can be increased if the vocabulary is drawn at first from the experiences of the learner, with new words and concepts introduced gradually in visual as well as oral presentations. New material should also be well organized and presented in a sequence beginning with simple, concrete items and proceeding to the complex and abstract segments. The use of diagrams, charts, pictures, and other visual aids may help the learner to perceive meaningfulness in unfamiliar material.

Appropriate Practice

The amount of practice is the most important factor in learning simple material. The more the learner practises, the better the material is learned. Mere repetition without purpose or guidance is of little value as it does not result in increased learning.

In most cases, short periods of practice followed by short rest intervals result in the best learning. This pattern is known as *distributed practice. Massed practice* involving long periods without interruption is usually not as effective in helping adults to learn. The less capable and less experienced the learner, the more he will benefit from distributed practice. Capable and experienced learners are more able to benefit from massed practice. Distributed practice is generally superior when the material is complex, of low meaningfulness, or when there is a large amount to be learned.

New material may be learned by practising either the whole or one part at a time. The *whole method* is usually preferred if performance after learning requires that the material be remembered as a unit. If that is not necessary, then learning by the *part method* of practice may prove to be superior, especially if the learner is inexperienced and the material is difficult or not very meaningful. There are no clear-cut guidelines to follow in choosing one method of practice over another, so a combination of the whole and part methods may achieve the best results in most cases.

Short practice sessions should be used at the beginning of a course, but the sessions may be lengthened as the learners gain experience. The goals for each practice period should be clearly understood by the learners, the learners should know the purpose of each activity, and the goals that are set should be capable of attainment by each learner. Group practice sessions should be used to introduce and establish a skill which can be developed further by individual practice tailored to the needs of each adult learner. Practice activities should be organized so that they appeal to as many of the senses as possible. In learning new terms, for example, repeating a word out loud in addition to reading it and writing it will result in better learning.

Reinforcement

Reinforcement is anything in the learning situation that increases the probability that the desired behaviour will be repeated. Reinforcement takes the form either of *reward* or *punishment,* and reward is usually more effective in helping adults to learn. Just as was the case with the principle of meaningful material, reinforcement depends upon the perception of the learner. If he sees the instructor's actions as being rewarding, then he will act on that basis. Sometimes, however, an intended reward is seen as a punishment by the learner if it singles him out from the learning group for special attention.

Although punishment is generally thought of as some form of physical action, the psychological meaning of the term includes more subtle acts by the instructor: a frown or the use of sarcasm or ridicule could be viewed by the learner as punishment. Punishment tends to be less effective than reward in bringing about learning since it is impossible to predict how the adult will react. It tells the learner that the behaviour was incorrect, but it does not always indicate the appropriate behaviour. In addition, punishment frequently produces unwanted side effects such as anger, fear, anxiety, or apathy in the learner.

Reward in a learning situation can also be subtle, involving such acts as a smile, a nod of the head, or a brief word of encouragement. When used to encourage learning, reward should be minimal rather than effusive praise. It should be just large enough to ensure that the appropriate behaviour will be repeated. A reward that is too large would be difficult to repeat in the future. Reward should be given as frequently as possible and should follow closely after the behaviour that is being rewarded, or the learner will tend to lose the connection between the behaviour and the reward.

Knowledge of Results

Learning is aided if the adult finds out immediately after practice whether or not his response was correct. This *feedback* or *knowledge of results* acts as reinforcement and is especially important to adult learners, who may have been away from a formal instructional setting for many years. Knowledge of results is provided fairly readily in psychomotor learning. In typing, for example, a key is struck and the results appear immediately on the paper. Knowledge of results is more difficult to provide with cognitive material, but can be done with frequent verbal guidance by the instructor. Another method of providing knowledge of results in cognitive learning is to use short, informal quizzes consisting of two or three items with the answers given immediately by the instructor while the learners correct their work. The informal quiz avoids the anxieties usually found with formal testing, and meets the special requirement for feedback as to learning progress.

> *Principles of learning:*
> 1. *Meaningful material*
> 2. *Appropriate practice*
> 3. *Reinforcement*
> 4. *Knowledge of results*

MEMORY

The process of learning new material is the first phase in a complex series of events leading to its eventual use in a new situation. The basic steps involved are learning the material, retaining it over a period of time, and retrieving it when called upon to do so. In greater detail, the sequence involves the seven stages outlined below.

1. The material is perceived and understood by the learner.
2. The material is held in short-term memory for a brief period.
3. A more permanent storage of the material is established.
4. The relatively permanent storage is maintained until the material is needed, although some changes may occur.
5. A new situation requiring use of the stored material is recognized.
6. The material is retrieved from amongst all the other material that is stored in memory.
7. The recalled material is used in the new situation.

Remembering is an active process whereby the effects of previous learning are displayed in the present. This may be accomplished either by *recall* of the material when past learning is recreated or reproduced, or by *recognition,* which involves identifying learned material when it is encountered again. As it is usually easier to recognize than to recall learned material, learners should be informed as to which type of memory is required for different material so they will know how to practise. If memory is to be tested, then varying types of test items are used depending upon the memory process involved. Short-answer and essay questions are used to test recall memory, while recognition is tested by true-false and multiple-choice questions.

Memory involves both a short-term and a long-term aspect. *Short-term memory* includes a time span of only a few seconds or minutes, yet it is a crucial period if new material is to be remembered. Only a small amount of material can be retained in short-term storage at any one time, with the average for adults consisting of 6 or 7 letters or 7 or 8 numbers, the approximate length of a telephone number. This relatively small amount is reduced even further if the learner shifts his attention to other things between the time that the original material is presented and the time that it is used. Rehearsing or practising the material should therefore begin early in the learning process if it must be retained in memory for any length of time.

Long-term memory varies considerably depending upon whether the recall or recognition method is involved. Figure 3 shows typical curves of remembering for various time periods. In every time interval up to two days, recognition remains at a much higher level than does recall.

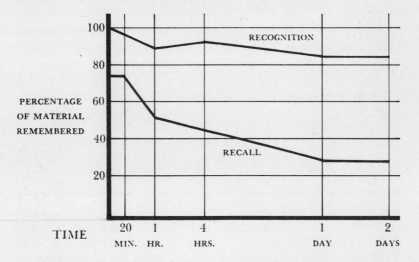

Figure 3. Long-Term Memory by Recall and Recognition

The amount of material that can be kept in long-term memory depends on the type and amount of the material, the ability of the learner, and the way in which the material was learned. Meaningful material is remembered better than non-meaningful material. A large amount of material requires a disproportionate time and effort compared to a small amount of material. To increase the ability to remember, material should be learned according to the principles of learning discussed previously. The material should also be reviewed occasionally to ensure that it is retained.

> *Types of Memory:*
> *1. Recall*
> *2. Recognition*
> *3. Short-term*
> *4. Long-term*

Not all material that is learned will be remembered. Forgetting seems most likely to occur immediately after learning; then there is a gradual reduction in the amount of material remembered over a period of time when cognitive material is involved. Forgetting may occur for several reasons:

1. New material may interfere with the recall of old material.

2. Old material may interfere with the retention of new material.

3. Material may be forgotten because the learner is no longer rewarded for the desired behaviour once he leaves the formal instructional setting.

4. Material that is unpleasant or threatening may be actively pushed out of the memory.

In order to reduce the amount of forgetting, the instructor should attempt to distinguish clearly among items that are to be learned so that the amount of interference is reduced. He should also ask the learner to practise beyond the point where recall is possible, so that when the process of forgetting occurs, the learner will still be able to remember the desired behaviour. To discourage situations of deliberate forgetting, the instructor should attempt to create a pleasant atmosphere and use materials that will not be perceived as threatening by the adult learner. Forgetting will also be reduced if the learned material can be transferred to a situation that the learner is likely to encounter in his everyday activities.

SETTING THE STAGE

Most adults engage in learning on a voluntary basis, so it is important that instruction be based on an understanding of how adults learn. If the participants decide that the learning experience is not satisfactory, they may withdraw from the educational programme and it will have failed. Therefore, in addition to meeting the basic requirements for adult learning outlined in this chapter, the formal instructional setting should be designed in keeping with other factors known to influence adult learning.

The climate established should be as relaxed and informal as possible so that no psychological barriers to learning develop. When the adult feels threatened or uncomfortable in a learning situation, his willingness to learn diminishes sharply. Since most people resist change and learning implies change, there will always be some element of discomfort in a learning situation. The instructor should attempt to reassure the adult that change is not necessarily harmful by relating new material to his needs and problems.

A successful learning experience requires considerable activity and involvement on the part of the adult participant. If learner activity is included as an integral part of an educational programme from the beginning, the successful instructor will be able to move gradually into the background as the learners accept responsibility for managing their own learning. In effect, adults can learn how to learn by learning.

CHAPTER ONE POST-ASSESSMENT

When you have read chapter one, complete the post-assessment shown below. Indicate whether each statement is true or false and show the degree of confidence in your answer.

Correctness of Statement
T The statement is true.
F The statement is false.

Degree of Confidence
1 I guessed at the answer.
2 My answer may be correct.
3 I'm confident that my answer is correct.

1. Changes in behaviour are an indication that learning has taken place. | T F 1 2 3
2. Learning in the formal instructional setting is usually less effective than learning in the natural societal setting. | T F 1 2 3
3. The length of a break does not affect the learning curve. | T F 1 2 3
4. The instructor of adults has direct control over the internal learning process of his students. | T F 1 2 3
5. Memorizing the names of the bones in the human body is an example of learning in the cognitive domain. | T F 1 2 3
6. Learning to play golf is an example of learning in the affective domain. | T F 1 2 3
7. Changing an attitude towards a minority group is an example of learning in the psychomotor domain. | T F 1 2 3
8. Reward is more effective than punishment in helping adults to learn. | T F 1 2 3
9. The part method of practice should be used when material must be remembered as a unit. | T F 1 2 3
10. It is easier to recognize than to recall learned material. | T F 1 2 3

The correct answers are given on the next page.

ANSWERS

1. T; 2. F; 3. F; 4. F; 5. T; 6. F; 7. F; 8. T; 9. F; 10. T

If you answered less than 8 items correctly, re-read chapter one carefully and try to apply the material to your own situation.

FOR FURTHER STUDY

1. Bass, Bernard M. and James A. Vaughan. *Training in Industry: The Management of Learning.* Belmont, California: Wadsworth Publishing Company, 1966. (paperback)

2. Hunter, I.M.L. *Memory.* Harmondsworth: Penguin Books, 1964. (paperback)

3. Mednick, Sarnoff A. *Learning.* Englewood Cliffs, New Jersey: Prentice-Hall, 1964. (paperback)

2

THE ADULT LEARNER: PRE-ASSESSMENT

Before reading chapter two, complete the pre-assessment test given below. Indicate whether the statements are true or false and the degree of confidence in your answer.

Correctness of Statement   Degree of Confidence

T The statement is true.   1 I guessed at the answer.

F The statement is false.   2 My answer may be correct.

                                               3 I'm confident that my answer is correct.

1. An adult's ability to learn is influenced by his occupation.   T F 1 2 3
2. Older students should be assigned to do more reading in order to catch up to younger students.   T F 1 2 3
3. The ability to hear reaches a peak at about age twenty-five.   T F 1 2 3
4. Age influences the speed of learning.   T F 1 2 3
5. The need for learning occurs only at certain stages in an adult's life.   T F 1 2 3
6. A major change in visual acuity occurs between age forty and fifty.   T F 1 2 3
7. Adults learn primarily for later in life rather than to solve current problems.   T F 1 2 3
8. Intrinsic motivation is provided mainly by the instructor.   T F 1 2 3
9. It is better to group adult students by educational level than by age.   T F 1 2 3
10. Longitudinal studies show that adult learning abilities decline consistently with advancing age.   T F 1 2 3

Please turn to the next page for the correct answers and score your chapter two pre-assessment.

ANSWERS

1. T; 2. F; 3. F; 4. T; 5. F; 6. T; 7. F; 8. F; 9. T; 10. F

If you had 9 or 10 correct answers and confidence levels of 2 and 3, skim read chapter two. If you had 7 or 8 correct answers and confidence levels of 1, 2, and 3, read the chapter carefully. If you had 6 or less correct answers and confidence levels of 1 and 2, study the chapter in detail and try to apply the material to your own instructing.

the adult learner

The learning accomplished by an adult in the formal instructional setting depends upon a complex variety of factors including the physical situation, the subject matter, the instruction provided, and the characteristics of the learner himself. Much more so than the child in school, the adult is influenced by his personal and social situation, which has the potential either to hinder or to aid him in the process of learning. To provide a useful and effective learning situation, the instructor must know about the adults he is teaching and how certain factors in their background may affect their learning in the formal instructional setting.

Many adults hold the opinion that they are unable to learn, and this belief can indeed prevent them from learning. Adult learning abilities tend to remain at a high level throughout life, although they are influenced by many factors including vision and hearing, education and occupation, and interests and attitudes. This chapter begins by examining adult learning abilities, then considers some of the factors that influence learning ability and performance. Guidelines for teachers of adults are given in each section.

GENERAL LEARNING ABILITY

The general learning ability of adults is usually measured by the total score received on an intelligence test. A number of psychologists have found that learning ability reaches a peak somewhere between age twenty and thirty, and then begins to decline. Others have disagreed, suggesting instead that the general learning ability of adults does not decline with age.

The earliest studies of adult intelligence were conducted by E.L. Thorndike, who reported in 1928 that the peak learning ability occurring between the ages of twenty and twenty-five was followed by a 13 to 15 per cent loss by age forty-two. Thorndike noted that general learning ability between age twenty-five and thirty-five was superior to that of childhood and equal or superior to that of early adolescence.

The brightest and dullest of people seemed to reach their peak at about the same age. Thorndike concluded that nobody under forty-five should restrain himself from trying to learn anything because of a belief or fear that he is too old to learn it, nor should he use that fear as an excuse for not learning anything which he ought to learn. If he fails to learn, inability due directly to age would rarely be the reason.

The curve of learning ability first reported by Thorndike has been found in other studies. Mental ability, as measured by the 1939 edition of the Wechsler individual intelligence test, grows rapidly from birth through puberty, then slows its growth in the early twenties until a slow but steady decline begins. In later editions of the Wechsler test, the age at which maximum scores are obtained has increased by about ten years. As shown in Figure 4, other studies using the army 'Alpha' test and the Otis intelligence test show the same general pattern of decline with age suggested by Wechsler.

Some psychologists have disagreed with the curve of general learning ability that shows a decline with age. Irving Lorge, for example, maintained that intelligence tests with rigid time limits discriminated against adults because they did not differentiate between *speed* of performance and the actual *ability* to do the tasks required by the test. Lorge developed an untimed test and found that when speed was not considered, there was no loss in general learning ability with age. The peak was reached around age twenty and the scores remained fairly consistent after that.

A second criticism of the studies showing a decline of intelligence with age is that they measured a cross-section of the adult population at one point in time, and did not take into account that the average schooling received by twenty-year olds would be more recent and much greater than that of sixty-year olds. To overcome this problem, several psychologists have conducted studies measuring the same individuals at several different periods in their lives. One such longitudinal study was reported by W.A. Owens, who first tested a group of college men in 1919, then retested them in 1950 and in 1961. The average test score of the ninety-six men who were tested three times increased from 5.7 to 6.3 be-

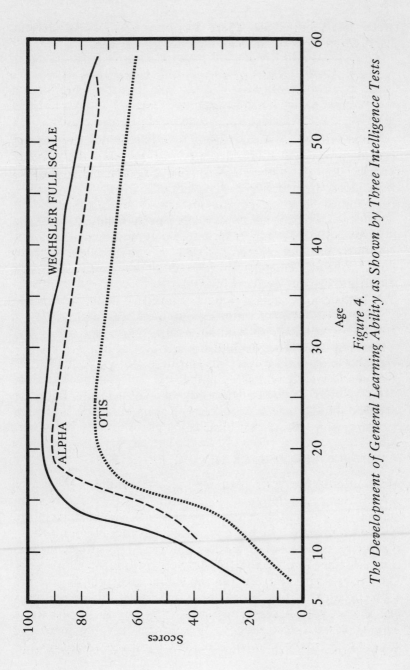

Figure 4.
The Development of General Learning Ability as Shown by Three Intelligence Tests

tween 1919 and 1950. There was only a slight decrease in 1961, when most of the men were in their sixties.

> *Adult learning performance is based upon:*
> *1. Power to learn.*
> *2. Speed of learning.*

There is no firm answer as to whether or not the general learning ability of adults declines with age, but the existing research provides some clues for planning and managing successful learning experiences for adults.

1. Almost anything can be learned at any age, providing that the instructional process is properly handled.

2. An adult may expect more rapid achievement than he is able to produce. Watch for signs of this problem because if it is not detected and corrected, the individual may become discouraged and frustrated.

3. Instructions and assignments should be planned with the speed capabilities of various group members in mind.

4. Older students should be permitted to set their own learning pace. They should be encouraged but not rushed.

5. Work of good quality should be expected, but production will take longer as age increases.

6. To help compensate for the slower learning rates of older adults, select a central idea or principle and plan instruction around that basic concept.

SPECIFIC LEARNING ABILITIES

Most intelligence tests that are used with adults consist of several sub-tests designed to measure specific abilities. In general, scores on sub-tests concerned with verbal or language abilities remain at a higher level as age advances than do those measuring non-verbal or manual abilities. This difference was quite distinct in a study of 2,000 Scottish industrial workers. On a vocabulary test used as the verbal measure, the average score increased from 50 points at age twenty to 58 points at age thirty, with a slight decrease to 54 points at age sixty. The non-verbal test used in the same study measured the capacity to make comparisons and to analyse logically. In this sub-test there was a steady decline from 50 points at age twenty to 30 points at age sixty.

In the longitudinal study conducted by Owens, scores on reasoning ability and verbal intelligence increased between 1919 and 1961 while numerical ability declined. Other studies have reported that judgement and reasoning reach their peaks later than other abilities. The sections of the Wechsler test that depend on the use of words and that draw upon experience show little decline with age.

The changing pattern of specific learning abilities has several implications for teachers of adults. Learning performance will vary with the type of material, so allow proportionately more time for teaching non-verbal skills than for verbal material involving language. The higher level of vocabulary, information and experience of older adults can help others in the group to learn, so their knowledge should be tapped in order to give greater depth to new material. Older students should be encouraged to relate new or difficult concepts to their existing knowledge.

FACTORS INFLUENCING LEARNING ABILITY

A number of social and economic characteristics influence the general and specific learning abilities of adults. Lorge found that the amount of formal education received was related to performance on an intelligence test. The average score on the army 'Alpha' test increased by more than 30 points between World War I and World War II, with most of the gain being attributed to a rise in the average schooling from 6.7 to 9.3 years in that same period. In another study, Lorge retested men in 1941 who had been tested in 1921 when they were in grade eight. He found that those who had completed their formal schooling received much higher intelligence-test scores than did those who had dropped out after the eighth grade. It seems, then, that the greater the amount of formal schooling, the greater the learning ability of adults. The amount of previous education is more important than age when assessing adult learning ability.

The occupation of the individual also seems to influence his specific learning abilities. People learn from what they do, so they acquire new knowledge and skills from their work. The meaningfulness and relevance of intelligence-test items to the occupation affects test scores; thus, clerical workers maintain a higher level of arithmetic ability than people who do not use such skills in their work. Adults with professional occupations generally increase their vocabularies up to about age seventy, but adults who do not use language extensively in their work experience a decline in vocabulary with age.

There are several steps the instructor can take in order to minimize the effects of education and occupation on the learning abilities of adults. Persons having a low education or who have been away from school for a long time should be given special attention and assistance in making adjustments to the new learning situation. The instruction given should also be made meaningful to the learners in terms of their occupational and cultural backgrounds. If an adult class must be divided into groups for instruction, then do so on the basis of educational or occupational similarities rather than by age.

Adult learning performance is influenced by:
1. *The type of material.*
2. *Previous education.*
3. *Occupation.*

PHYSIOLOGICAL CHANGES

The way that humans change as they grow older affects the amount of new material they can learn and the speed at which they learn it. Instruction must therefore be modified to suit the characteristics of the learners, and this is particularly important in the psychomotor domain where speed of performance is critical. Changes in such capacities as vision and hearing occur quite naturally throughout the adult years, and the nature and pace of instruction should be adapted to the abilities of adult learners in these areas.

Considerable research has been done on the physiological changes that occur with aging and how these affect learning, with the first systematic study being done by Sir Francis Galton in 1884. At a fair held in South Kensington, England,

Galton set up a booth and collected measurements from more than 7,000 volunteers. He measured seventeen different characteristics including height, weight, vision, and hearing. Following Galton's original study, many others have tested adults of different ages. The general pattern is for most physiological capacities to reach a peak near age twenty, and then decline gradually as age advances. The curve of change for most physiological characteristics is similar to that shown in Figure 4 for adult learning ability.

Vision

As much as 85 per cent of all learning occurs through the use of the eyes, so the proper functioning of vision is quite important in an instructional situation. There is a steady decline with age in the efficiency of all visual functions, even in eyes that are otherwise normal and healthy. The ability to see distinctly reaches a maximum around age eighteen. As can be seen in Figure 5, the decline in vision is fairly steady from age twenty to forty, but then there is a sharp drop between age forty and fifty.

The range of clear vision becomes narrower with advancing age. The near point of vision, or the distance at which detailed material can be seen clearly, is about 4 inches at age twenty compared to 9 inches at age forty and 16 inches at age fifty. Thus, the older an adult becomes, the farther away from his eyes he must hold a book or newspaper when reading.

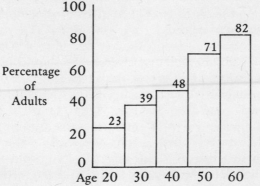

Figure 5. Percentage of Adults Having Defective Vision

The far point of vision, or the distance at which far-away objects can be seen clearly, moves closer as age advances. As a result, the visual field becomes narrower, and correction with reading glasses is necessary for most people by the time they reach fifty years of age.

The pupil of a person aged fifty admits only half as much light as at age twenty. Older people therefore require more illumination to perform tasks involving vision. If a person twenty years old required 100 watts of light to perform a visual task, a sixty-year-old would need 230 watts in order to perform the same task. The rate of poor colour vision rises with age. One study examined 1,000 adults of all ages and found that 11 per cent of the men and 6 per cent of the women had poor colour vision. Finally, the speed of seeing slows down with advancing age and it becomes more difficult for an adult to shift from looking at something close to something far away. Changing focus from looking at the instructor or the chalkboard to writing notes or reading takes an increasingly longer time as age increases.

Changes in vision as age advances:
1. Incidence of defective vision increases.
2. Range of clear vision narrows.
3. Pupil of the eye admits less light.
4. Visual reaction time slows down.

A number of ways in which an instructor can help the learner to compensate for the declines in vision that occur with age are listed below.

1. Adequate illumination for the age level of the students should be provided. The light source should be constant, without flicker, and the learners shouldn't face direct light. Glare should be reduced or eliminated if possible.

2. If visual attention to fine detail is required, rooms should be equipped with work stations having supplementary light sources which can be operated by the individual.

3. Watch for signs of visual performance problems such as fatigue, loss of attention, or frequent shifts in the position of reading materials.

4. Try to avoid requiring students to make sudden or fre-

quent changes of focus. Assist them in locating the desired point of focus before continuing a presentation.

5. Seating should be arranged close to the instructor or illustrative material so that everyone can see clearly.

6. Charts, diagrams, or pictures should be large, with maximum colour contrast. Allow sufficient time for the presentation of visual materials so that the students don't feel too rushed.

7. Chalkboards or large paper pads used by the instructor should allow maximum contrast. A white plastic board with black lithographic chalk provides the best contrast.

8. If a chalkboard is used, only important and relevant items should appear. Use simple words or phrases and large, legible writing or printing.

9. Reading materials should be printed on low gloss paper in large type with double spacing. Mimeograph or offset processes are preferable to 'ditto' reproductions, which usually have poor colour contrast.

10. The amount of reading expected should be reduced for older students.

Hearing

Loss of hearing during the adult years is usually gradual and may not be noticed by the individual. Nevertheless, a hearing loss may result in problems of communication that hinder learning. Maximum hearing ability occurs between ten and fifteen years of age, after which there is a gradual but consistent decline to age sixty-five. As Figure 6 shows, about one-eighth of the twenty-year-olds have defective hearing compared to half of the sixty-year-old group. The most rapid decline occurs between ages fifty and sixty.

The ability to hear sounds is important when teaching adults, but even more crucial is the ability to distinguish one particular sound from among many other interfering sounds. Discrimination of sound is affected by a number of age-related factors, and the ability to discriminate and comprehend speech is reduced sharply by the presence of other sounds as age advances. Men tend to lose the ability to hear high-pitched sounds, while women become less able to hear low-pitched sounds.

As with visual reaction time, auditory reaction time also slows down with advancing age. An older person has difficulty in comprehending rapid speech, even if there is little or no hearing loss.

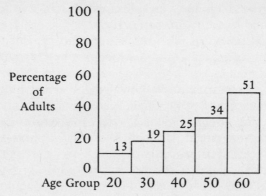

Figure 6. Percentage of Adults Having Defective Hearing

> *Changes in hearing as age advances:*
> *1. Incidence of defective hearing increases.*
> *2. Sound discrimination decreases.*
> *3. Auditory reaction time slows down.*

There are a number of things an instructor can do to offset the hearing defects that are bound to be present in any group of adult students.

1. Try to eliminate or reduce outside noises, such as air conditioning or heating elements, that may distract or interfere with hearing.

2. Remain in one position as much as possible so that the listeners can observe gestures which may provide clues to meaning.

3. Speak slowly, distinctly, and clearly. Shouting only increases the overtones and echoes in the room and makes hearing more difficult.

4. Talk directly to the students in a conversational manner, using simple words and short sentences.

5. Watch the faces of the students for clues as to whether or not they can hear. Ask someone at the back of the room to call attention if he suspects that someone can't hear.

6. Questions directed from the group to the instructor should be repeated so that everyone can hear them.

7. Use a chalkboard or some other device to show new or unfamiliar words visually. The use of an overhead projector would enable you to remain facing the listeners so that those who need to can lip-read.

8. Individual work stations should be provided with devices for augmenting sound which can be controlled by the student.

9. Smaller rooms are better than larger ones as they reduce sound reflection. Use small, private discussion rooms if possible rather than having several groups in one room.

10. Students with a hearing loss will respond better and feel less isolated or threatened in small groups than in large ones.

11. Group discussions for older students should be slower-paced than those conducted for younger adults. Frequent summaries will also help the older members keep up. Pause often to allow for the correlation of ideas.

Other Changes

Changes in vision and hearing affect learning the most, but numerous other physiological developments occur as aging progresses. It becomes more difficult for the body to adjust to both high and low external temperatures, which is particularly important when there is a wide age range in a group. The strength of the biceps decreases, bones become more fragile, and the capacity for cell growth and tissue repair becomes retarded. In addition, there is a gradual over-all loss of energy as age advances, and various motor abilities, such as strength of pull, decrease.

One of the characteristics that Galton studied was reaction speed. If the reaction speed at age twenty-five was 100 per cent, comparable figures at age thirty-five and forty-five would be 99 and 96 per cent. Later studies observed a similar pattern, with fairly rapid declines beyond the forties.

The instructor can do several things to minimize the effects of such physiological changes.

1. Pay close attention to the physical environment. Room temperature and ventilation should be adjusted to suit the age of the learners.

2. Courses should be planned within the speed capabilities of the majority of learners, particularly when motor skills are to be learned.

3. Older students should be permitted to choose their own work tempo. They should be encouraged and stimulated but not rushed.

4. Assignments should not be so long as to frustrate the students. Long assignments can often be reduced by staying on the main points.

5. Unnecessary routines, such as rushing from room to room in order to meet arbitrary deadlines, should be eliminated as they lead to early fatigue.

6. A pleasant social atmosphere will help to relieve many of the anxieties and tensions felt by students regarding their physical capabilities.

Other physiological changes accompanying aging:
1. *A gradual slowing of bodily functions.*
2. *Greater difficulty adapting to temperature changes.*
3. *Decline in reaction speed.*
4. *Over-all loss of energy.*

PSYCHOLOGICAL TRENDS

The concept of *differentiation* is important in understanding the psychological condition of adult learners. As a person moves through the adult years, his psychological characteristics become intensified and he becomes more differentiated in relation to other people. A pre-adult learning group in school has an age range of about two years, few students have job experience, and all of them are studying the same subject. An adult learning group, however, may have an age range of fifty years, a great variety of experience in many kinds of jobs, and markedly different learning interests. Family responsibilities may range from single persons to married adults with several children, while educational background can vary from no schooling to university graduation within a single group of learners. Within an adult group, there is a much wider range of interests, attitudes, motivations, and skills, than would be found in a group of young people. As a result, the instructor will have difficulty in organizing learning experiences for the group as a whole. He must work as much as possible with individuals or small groups where the learning interests and needs are quite specific.

Other psychological trends help to differentiate between children and adults, and these suggest ways of designing learning programmes for an adult group.

1. Young people see themselves as dependent on others, but adults view themselves as independent, responsible, and self-directing persons. The instructor should therefore help adults discover for themselves what they need to learn and guide them in planning and conducting their own learning activities.

2. Adults have more experiences and more varied kinds of experiences upon which they can base the learning of new material than young people. The instructor should use teaching techniques that draw upon that experience, using illustrations and examples from the learner's own background whenever possible.

3. Youths learn for later in life, but adults are more concerned about the immediate application of new material to the solution of their current problems. Material should be organized around those problems rather than by subjects or topics.

Adult learners:
1.   *Are highly differentiated.*
2.   *View themselves as independent persons.*
3.   *Have a wide variety of experiences.*
4.   *Are concerned with immediate problems.*

INTERESTS

Interests are psychological factors within an individual which attract him or repel him from various objects, persons, and activities within his environment. We often say that a student 'isn't really interested' in the subject we are teaching, and we reach this conclusion about his likes and dislikes by listening to his expressions of how he feels and by watching his behaviour.

Edward K. Strong, a pioneer in the study of adult interests, found that the things liked most at age twenty-five are liked better and better with increasing age. On the other hand, the things liked least at age twenty-five are liked less and less as age increases. Older men have as many likes and dislikes as younger men, but their interests are different. Interests suggesting skill and daring such as climbing mountains or racing cars show the greatest change, with older men not liking these activities as much as younger men. Older men do not like activities that involve change or interference with established habits and customs. In most cases, the liking for occupations decreases with age. Interest in activities involving speaking or writing decreases with age, but interest in reading tends to increase. Older men prefer those kinds of activities that can be done alone rather than those involving others, and they are usually surer of their estimates of themselves than are younger men.

Changes in interests do not occur at the same rate throughout life, according to Strong. About 50 per cent of the total change occurs between ages twenty-five and thirty-five, 20 per cent between thirty-five and forty-five, and 30 per cent between forty-five and fifty-five. There is very little change after age fifty-five. Changes in interest from year to year are not great, and age is not as important an influence on interest change as is occupation. Changes that occur are related more to a person's occupation than to his age.

E.L. Thorndike was also an early student of adult interests. He found that the interests needed to support adult learning showed no decrease with age, and that interests could be modified through learning. Thorndike also discovered that older adults are more influenced than younger adults by material that they regarded as useless or harmful. The older student would need 10 to 20 per cent more time to learn useless material than he would to learn things he regarded as fairly useful.

As age increases, the interests of adults:
1. *Tend to crystallize.*
2. *Transfer to different topics.*
3. *Support learning.*

Very little learning can occur without some degree of interest. If you observe a class closely, you will be able to detect topics that the adult students are interested in and those in which they have little interest. For those topics where interest is high, there shouldn't be too much difficulty in helping adults to learn. If interest is low, however, a more imaginative approach to instruction is necessary. Try to develop interest by showing the relationship of the uninteresting material to the more interesting topics. Intersperse the less interesting topics among the more interesting ones so that there is no long sequence of uninteresting subject matter. In teaching theory, try to show the practical applications wherever possible, as this will help to create interest. Interest can also be developed by creating situations in which success can be achieved by the adult student.

ATTITUDES

The term *attitude* is much more difficult to define than the term interest. An attitude involves three things: an object, a set of beliefs, and a tendency to behave. The attitude object is the thing about which we hold an attitude. The set of beliefs indicates whether we feel that the object is good or bad, and the tendency to behave leads us to act so as to keep or get rid of the object.

There are additional aspects of attitudes that the instructor should consider. How intensely does a person feel about the attitude object? How much knowledge does he have about it? How resistant is he to changing his attitude? If an attitude is high in intensity and knowledge, then there is a good chance of predicting a person's behaviour. For example, if you have a strongly favourable attitude towards a particular make of car and considerable knowledge of cars, then you would probably purchase that make of car.

> *In analysing adult attitudes, consider:*
> 1. *Intensity of the attitude.*
> 2. *Level of knowledge.*
> 3. *Resistance to change.*

As people grow older, their attitudes tend to become more

stable and fixed, and therefore more difficult to change. Attitude change can only occur if people are placed in a situation where change can take place, and where the desired attitude can be demonstrated. If the goals of a course include changing attitudes toward neatness, punctuality, and customer relations, then instruction must be designed so that such changes are encouraged and practised. Lecturing is a very poor way of attempting to change attitudes because people tend to ignore communications that conflict with their existing attitudes. Teaching techniques such as role-playing and group discussion force adults into examining their existing attitudes, which is necessary before change can occur.

Even if the goals of a course don't include changing attitudes, those kinds of change will occur. The instructor's standards and conduct provide a model which students will imitate. The instructor's attitudes about the subject being taught are readily apparent and may be learned by the students.

DEVELOPMENTAL TASKS

Childhood is viewed as a developmental period during which a person grows physically, develops his personality, and learns to perform a role in society. This growth is often thought to stop once adulthood is reached, but Robert Havighurst has suggested that adulthood is also a developmental period during which certain kinds of further growth occur. During adulthood, *developmental tasks* arise. The tasks are the same for almost every adult, and they are centred around social and cultural activities. According to Havighurst, successful achievement of the developmental tasks will lead to happiness and success with later tasks, while failure leads to unhappiness in the individual, disapproval by society, and difficulty with later tasks.

The life of the adult consists of three general developmental periods: early adulthood, from eighteen to thirty; middle age, from age thirty to fifty-five; and later maturity, from age fifty-five onwards. Different developmental tasks arise in each period in an adult's life. In early adulthood the tasks include:

1. Selecting a mate.
2. Learning to live with the marriage partner.
3. Starting a family.
4. Rearing children.
5. Managing a home.
6. Getting started in an occupation.
7. Taking a civic responsibility.
8. Finding a congenial group.

The developmental tasks during middle age include:
1. Achieving civic and social responsibility.
2. Establishing and maintaining an economic standard of living.
3. Assisting children to become adults.
4. Developing leisure-time activities.
5. Relating to one's spouse as a person.
6. Accepting and adjusting to changes of middle age.
7. Adjusting to aging parents.

The new developmental tasks in later maturity include:
1. Adjusting to decreasing physical strength and health.
2. Adjusting to retirement and reduced income.
3. Adjusting to death of the spouse.
4. Establishing an affiliation with one's age group.
5. Meeting social and civic obligations.
6. Establishing satisfactory physical living arrangements.

Each developmental task involves a learning component, regardless of whether the learning occurs in the natural societal or the formal instructional setting. As each new task arises, a *teachable moment* occurs in which the adult is highly motivated and willing to learn. In some cases the educational programme may deal directly with the developmental tasks, so that motivation is high. In other instances, new material can be related to specific developmental tasks in order to increase the probability of learning.

MOTIVATION

Several different kinds of motivation can be observed in a learning situation. The adult must first be motivated to attend a course so that he will be in a position where instruction can be given. Once a person attends, then motivation to engage in learning is necessary, which means that the adult must be aware and attentive before he can start to learn. Finally, the adult student must be motivated so that he will continue to learn.

A distinction is often made between *intrinsic* and *extrinsic* sources of motivation. Intrinsic sources of motivation derive from within the individual and include curiosity, the desire to master a subject, need for achievement, and striving for knowledge for its own sake. Extrinsic motivation is usually provided by an instructor, through his use of reward and punishment of learning behaviours.

Several intrinsic-motivation techniques can be used in the formal instructional setting. The instructor should stress the future use or value of new material by using problems similar to those encountered on the job. He should also provide students with feedback throughout their learning so that they will know the extent of their progress towards the final goals of the course. New material should be related to interesting things already learned outside as well as inside the course. In following along a particular line of thought, maintain suspense as to the conclusion until all the facts have been considered.

With regard to extrinsic-motivation techniques in the classroom, reward is usually more effective than punishment in helping people to learn, as noted earlier. Punishment may produce undesirable side effects such as fear, anxiety, or hostility. In addition, punishment tends to focus too much attention on wrong responses, and it gives no indication as to what the correct response is.

> *Motivation may be:*
> 1. *Intrinsic.*
> 2. *Extrinsic.*

The motivation of most adult learners consists of varying degrees of both intrinsic and extrinsic elements, and both sources tend to decline somewhat with advancing age. Try to develop the intrinsic sources as much as possible so that the student can be freed from dependence on the instructor for his motivation. This will prepare him for the conditions he will probably encounter when he uses the learned material after leaving the formal instructional setting.

CHAPTER TWO POST-ASSESSMENT

When you have read chapter two, complete the post-assessment shown below. Indicate whether the statements are true or false and the degree of confidence in your answer.

Correctness of Statement
T The statement is true.
F The statement is false.

Degree of Confidence
1 I guessed at the answer.
2 My answer may be correct.
3 I'm confident that my answer is correct.

1. The concept of developmental tasks provides a way of identifying the educational needs of adults.	T F 1 2 3
2. Changes in adult interests occur uniformly throughout life.	T F 1 2 3
3. It is better to group adult students by age than by type of occupation.	T F 1 2 3
4. The instructor should try to develop extrinsic sources of motivation more than intrinsic sources.	T F 1 2 3
5. Non-verbal learning abilities tend to decline more rapidly than verbal abilities.	T F 1 2 3
6. Adult learning ability is influenced by the amount of formal education received.	T F 1 2 3
7. The near point of vision tends to move closer as age advances.	T F 1 2 3
8. About 50 per cent of all learning occurs through the use of the eyes.	T F 1 2 3
9. Auditory reaction time increases as age advances.	T F 1 2 3
10. The efficiency of mental operations is not affected by age.	T F 1 2 3

The correct answers are given on the next page.

ANSWERS

1. T; 2. F; 3. F; 4. F; 5. T; 6. T; 7. F; 8. F; 9. T; 10. F

If you had less than 8 correct answers, re-read chapter two carefully and try to obtain some of the references listed below.

FOR FURTHER STUDY

1. Bischof, L.J. *Adult Psychology.* Scranton, Pennsylvania: Harper and Row, 1969. (paperback)

2. Kidd, J.R. *How Adults Learn.* New York: Association Press, 1959.

3. Pressey, Sidney L. and Raymond G. Kuhlen. *Psychological Development Through the Life Span.* New York: Harper and Brothers, 1957.

3

COURSE PLANNING: PRE-ASSESSMENT

Before reading chapter three, complete the pre-assessment test given below. Indicate whether each statement is true or false, and the degree of confidence in your answer.

Correctness of Statement
T The statement is true.
F The statement is false.

Degree of Confidence
1 I guessed at the answer.
2 My answer may be correct.
3 I'm confident that my answer is correct.

1.	The objectives used in planning instruction should be used for informing others about your instructional intentions.	T F 1 2 3
2.	Behavioural objectives in the cognitive domain are the most difficult to write.	T F 1 2 3
3.	Terminal behaviour is the behaviour that the learner should be able to demonstrate at the beginning of instruction.	T F 1 2 3
4.	The goals of an educational programme should be stated in broad, general terms.	T F 1 2 3
5.	The following objective is expressed in behavioural terms: "The learner will list three major principles of instruction."	T F 1 2 3
6.	The following objective is non-behavioural: "When given two objectives, the learner will be able to identify correctly the one which is stated in behavioural terms."	T F 1 2 3
7.	Informing participants of the behavioural objectives for a course will not affect their learning.	T F 1 2 3
8.	Learning tasks should proceed from the familiar to the unknown.	T F 1 2 3
9.	Behavioural objectives in the psychomotor domain are the easiest to write.	T F 1 2 3
10.	Evaluation procedures should be designed before a course begins.	T F 1 2 3

Please turn to the next page for the correct answers and score your chapter three pre-assessment.

ANSWERS

1. F; 2. F; 3. F; 4. T; 5. T; 6. F; 7. F; 8. T; 9. T; 10. T

If you had 9 or 10 correct answers and confidence levels of 2 and 3, skim over chapter three. If you had 7 or 8 correct answers and confidence levels of 1, 2, and 3, read the chapter carefully. If you had 6 or less correct answers and confidence levels of 1 and 2, study the chapter in detail and try to think through the applications of the material to your own instructing.

course planning

The planning of programmes and courses may be the most important part of teaching adults. This aspect of instruction is often done poorly, in part because the effort involved is usually not visible to others and the work is generally unpaid. Many courses seem to be planned on the spur of the moment, which leads to confusion and uncertainty both for the instructor and for the adult learners. The instructor tends to select the subject matter he is most familiar with and uses techniques with which he feels most comfortable, without considering the needs and desires of the adult learners.

Little attention is paid in the planning of most courses to the desired behaviours of the learner at the end of the course. This aspect, however, is the central concept of course planning since the purpose of educational programmes is to produce some type of change in the learner. A *course* is a series of related activities or sessions conducted in a formal instructional setting and designed to produce specific changes in adult learners.

THE PLANNING PROCESS

Any course for adults can be planned in a systematic fashion if certain procedures are followed. By following a systematic method of planning, most decisions about course content and instructional procedures can be made in advance of starting the actual course. The method of course planning suggested here begins with a description of the potential participants in the course and the behaviours they must exhibit after they leave the course and return to their everyday situation. Those stages are followed by a more detailed analysis of the behaviours that must be learned during the course, with the product of this analysis forming an outline of the course content. Instructional processes are then selected that seem to offer the most effective way of teaching each part of the course, and methods of evaluating the instruction are determined.

In outline form, the seven elements in course planning are as follows:

1. *Performance analysis.*
Description and analysis of the job, task, or skill that an adult will be expected to perform once he has completed the course.

2. *Participant description.*
Detailed description of the characteristics of the potential participants in the course.

3. *Course goals.*
A brief statement in broad terms of the goals or purposes of the course.

4. *Behavioural objectives.*
Statements of the specific behaviours that must be learned in order to achieve the course goals.

5. *Learning tasks.*
A detailed listing of the sequence of learner activities leading to achievement of an objective.

6. *Instructional processes.*
Identification of the instructional techniques and devices that offer the greatest probability for successful achievement of each objective.

7. *Evaluation procedures.*
Determining the procedures that will be followed in order to assess the success of instruction in reaching the course goals and objectives.

> *Seven elements in course planning:*
> 1. *Performance analysis.*
> 2. *Participant description.*
> 3. *Course goals.*
> 4. *Behavioural objectives.*
> 5. *Learning tasks.*
> 6. *Instructional processes.*
> 7. *Evaluation procedures.*

The seven elements listed above constitute a *course plan*

which provides a comprehensive guide for the instructor in directing the learning activities of adults in a specific course. The course plan should not be viewed as inflexible or unalterable, but should be adapted to the needs of the group. There are few instances when the actual participants will correspond exactly to the potential participants envisioned during the planning process. Some of the behavioural objectives may be irrelevant to a specific group, while other groups may require or demand an augmented course. Insofar as possible, individual differences should be considered so that adults may begin the course at different levels and proceed at different rates, since some participants may already have achieved some of the predetermined objectives while others may need additional instruction.

PERFORMANCE ANALYSIS

The initial step in the course-planning process is to prepare a description and analysis of the job or skill that the potential participant will be expected to perform when he completes the course. This will provide the instructor with a clear picture of the real situation in which the learner must operate after receiving instruction. The complexity and difficulty of performance analysis varies with the type of course being planned.

When planning a course designed to teach specific job skills, two elements are necessary for performance analysis. A *job description* should be sought first; if none exists, one should be written. The job description states in one or two paragraphs what the person holding a position is required to do. A *list of duties* is developed from the job description and from observation of and discussion with persons performing the job. The list of duties should note in considerable detail all of the actions or tasks that the holder of the job performs. When the duties have been listed, the instructor should estimate how often each task is performed and how difficult the task is to learn.

> *Elements in performance analysis:*
> 1. *Job description.*
> 2. *List of duties.*

A similar procedure can be followed in analysing the behaviours that will be learned in a non-vocational course, whether it be basket weaving, bridge, public speaking, or English composition. The important aspect to consider is the use that will be made of the learned material after instruction has been completed. First, attempt to describe the situations in which performance of the learned behaviours will take place (job description); then identify the specific actions that are involved in performance (list of duties).

The performance analysis should be reviewed periodically so that the course can be kept up to date with current realities. Valuable sources of information for updating include conversations with people who work in the course-content area, reading current literature in the field, and maintaining contact with previous participants in the course.

PARTICIPANT DESCRIPTION

The second stage in the course-planning process is to describe as completely as possible the adults who might participate in the educational programme. This involves estimating the probable number of participants as well as describing in detail their characteristics. These estimates are useful in publicizing the course, developing prerequisites for the course, and in designing the specific learning activities that will be conducted for participants. Fairly accurate descriptions of potential participants can be obtained by analysing the characteristics of people who took similar courses in the past or from questions included on a pre-registration form completed by those who register in advance.

Any information that can be obtained about the potential participants will be useful in planning a course, but certain kinds of data are more helpful than others. Information should be sought in at least the following five general categories:

1. *Physical characteristics.*
This category is especially significant when a skill is to be learned. Characteristics such as height, weight, co-ordination, or appearance may help or prevent an adult from learning a skill and may influence his ability to perform the skill satisfactorily once it is learned.

2. *Personal characteristics.*

The age, sex, marital status, and other personal characteristics of the adult will influence his ability to learn new material as well as affect the use of the material when instruction has been completed.

3. *Educational experience.*

In this category consider both the level of education received by the adult and his subsequent experiences in continuing his education. People with a higher level of education together with considerable participation in adult-education activities will have greater ease in learning new material than those with a low level of education and little subsequent effort to continue their education. Try to determine whether or not the potential participants have taken courses in content areas similar to the present course.

4. *Occupational background.*

Information about present and previous jobs as well as occupational aspirations may provide clues to the motivation of the adult for taking a vocational course and help to establish the relevance of his skills to the content of a non-vocational course.

5. *Psychological characteristics.*

Determining some of the interests, attitudes, and motivations of the potential participants will help in designing learning activities that will be appealing and useful to them. A question like "Why do you want to take this course?" will enable the instructor to obtain some information about the psychological characteristics of the participants.

Categories of participant information:
1. *Physical characteristics.*
2. *Personal characteristics.*
3. *Educational experience.*
4. *Occupational background.*
5. *Psychological characteristics.*

COURSE GOALS

The statement of course goals represents a merging of the

performance analysis and participant description into a general statement of who the course is designed for and the areas of content that will be included. The goals or purposes of a course are usually expressed in one or two sentences and are phrased in general terms. For example, the goal of an introductory course for teachers of adults might be stated as follows: "To provide the participants with an introduction to the processes of learning and instruction in adult education so that they can improve the effectiveness of their educational programmes." The title of a course is usually derived from the statement of goals. The course mentioned above was titled "Teaching Adults: An Introductory Course."

The goals of a course are determined not only by the instructor but also by other sources that are concerned with the particular course or with that course as one element in a curriculum of courses. Statements of course goals are useful in determining the particular content area to be included in a specific course and help to prevent duplication or omission when several courses are to be presented. The preparation and description of goals for a particular course may therefore involve other instructors, programme administrators, and representatives of community organizations that have an interest in the programme.

A concise statement of course goals should be made available to potential participants before they enroll in a course so that they can determine whether or not it will meet their needs and expectations. An inaccurate or misleading statement of goals may result in dissatisfaction with the course and a high drop-out rate.

> *A statement of course goals should be:*
> 1. *Brief (one or two sentences).*
> 2. *Accurate.*
> 3. *Descriptive of the purposes of the course.*

BEHAVIOURAL OBJECTIVES

A clear statement of course objectives is crucial to successful course planning, since this stage identifies the specific things to be learned by the participants. Behavioural objectives are determined by referring to the course goals and the performance analysis. Satisfactory completion of the objectives results in the learner reaching the goals of the course.

In preparing course objectives, the focus is on the visible activities of the learner, which are referred to as *behaviours*. An objective, therefore, represents the pattern of behaviour that the learner should be able to demonstrate. The emphasis in preparing behavioural objectives is on *terminal behaviour*, or behaviour that the instructor would like the learner to be able to demonstrate upon completion of instruction.

Behavioural objectives are used for two purposes: to assist in planning instruction, and for communication with others. Each of the two functions requires a different type of behavioural objective. *Planning objectives* are used by the instructor to help him plan a course and are quite detailed. *Informational objectives* are less detailed since they are used in communicating the course objectives to the learners, to other instructors, and to programme administrators. A list of informational objectives should accompany the statement of course goals given to potential participants before they enroll in a course. The objectives should also be discussed and modified if necessary in the first session of the course.

> *Types of behavioural objectives:*
> *1. Planning objectives*
> *2. Informational objectives*

Planning objectives consist of five basic elements. The example shown below, which was used in an introductory course for teachers of adults, is analysed in parentheses following each of the five basic elements.

Planning objective. In a quiz given in the formal instructional setting, the learner will write three planning objectives for a course that he teaches and each example must include the five elements of a planning objective.

Elements
1. *Who* is to perform the behaviour. (the learner)
2. The *actual behaviour* to be used in demonstrating the behaviour. (writing)

3. The *result* of the behaviour. (three planning objectives for a course that he teaches)

4. The important *conditions* under which the behaviour must be demonstrated. (in a quiz given in the formal instructional setting)

5. The *standard* of performance required. (each example must include the five elements of a planning objective)

Informational objectives are less specific and detailed than planning objectives but they must succeed in communicating the intent of the instructor. Action terms such as write, list, identify, and describe should be used. Imprecise terms such as understand, know, and appreciate should be avoided as they do not refer to observable behaviours. The minimum elements in an informational objective are the type of behaviour and the product that is desired. An informational objective related to the planning objective discussed previously is shown below.

Informational objective. To write planning objectives for a course that you teach.

Elements
1. The *type of behaviour.* (writing)
2. The desired *product.* (planning objectives for a course that you teach)

The difficulty of writing behavioural objectives varies with the domain of learning involved. The psychomotor domain is the easiest to work with because all of the behaviours to be learned are readily observable, either while the action is being performed or as a product resulting from performance. Objectives in the cognitive domain are of intermediate difficulty to prepare. At the lower levels of the cognitive domain, the recall or use of learned material is emphasized. Behaviours such as producing a new communication or making judgements are emphasized at the higher levels of the cognitive domain. Objectives in the affective domain are the most difficult to write and may be stated either in non-measurable terms or in terms of the actual behaviour that the instructor intends to observe. An objective stating that the learner will become more interested in a topic is basically non-measurable, or a related objective could be observed in terms of an increase in the number of library books about the topic that are taken out by the learners.

The most difficult problem to overcome in preparing behavioural objectives is that of thinking in terms of instructor activities or traditional content areas rather than in terms of learner behaviours. Always begin by considering what the learner must do to demonstrate that he has learned. Once the behavioural objectives have been prepared, make sure that the learners know and understand them, as this will result in more effective learning.

> *Behavioural objectives should be:*
> 1. *Written in terms of observable behaviours.*
> 2. *Clear statements of the instructor's intent.*
> 3. *Communicated to the learner.*

LEARNING TASKS

When the behavioural objectives for a course have been determined, each of them is analysed in terms of *learning tasks*, which are the things that must be done in order to achieve the objective. The learning tasks that are identified are arranged in the sequence in which they must be learned. This process of identifying and ordering learning tasks results in an outline of the course content.

The learning tasks needed to achieve an objective are cumulative and form a hierarchy. Unless a learner is able to master the first task, he is unable to learn the second, and if he doesn't learn the second, he can't learn the third. Success with the first task, however, gives him an opportunity to complete the second, and achieving the second task means that he can tackle the third. The ordering of the learning tasks is therefore of crucial importance. If one is omitted either in the planning stage or during instruction, the possibility of the learner achieving the behavioural objective is greatly reduced.

When the learning tasks are identified and placed in the most suitable order, the learners should be assessed at the beginning of the course to determine where each person stands in relation to the learning tasks and behavioural objectives. If this is done, it will be necessary to arrange individual programmes of instruction as much as possible since different learners will be at different levels. Some will have mastered some or all of the tasks required to achieve an objective, while others may not have any previous knowledge. Assessment at the beginning of the course provides the instructor with information that enables him to provide the most appropriate instruction for each learner, thus saving considerable time and effort. He does not need to provide instruction for tasks that the students have already mastered, and he is able to give additional instruction in tasks where the learners have difficulty.

The number and type of learning tasks vary greatly for different behavioural objectives, so there are no specific steps to follow in determining how many and what kinds of tasks to list. Each behavioural objective must be carefully analysed to ensure that the best possible sequence is designed. Experience does, however, suggest some general guidelines for the arrangement of learning tasks in order to provide the most effective instruction possible.

1. *General to specific.*
Learning tasks are more clearly established in the mind of the learner if they proceed from general to specific. Once the student has an overview of the content and understands what is expected, he can then learn the specific details and relate them to the desired end product or behaviour.

2. *Concrete to abstract.*
Learning tasks are more readily understood if they proceed from concrete to abstract. Practical applications should be demonstrated before the student attempts to learn theory. In this way, he is able to see a concrete, meaningful use for theory that might be difficult to learn because it is abstract and not meaningful in itself.

3. *Familiar to unknown.*
The learning tasks presented early in a course should be related to and draw upon the previous experiences of the learners. Later in the course, unknown material can be introduced and related to the familiar.

4. *Scatter interesting tasks.*

The motivation of learners can be maintained by beginning with a learning task that is highly interesting and by placing other interesting tasks at scattered intervals throughout the course. The most interesting learning tasks can usually be identified the first time that the course is taught, since they are difficult to determine in advance.

5. *Logical order.*

In some cases the order of performance determines a logical sequence for learning tasks. In learning to drive, for example, the student must know how to stop a car before learning how to steer under road conditions.

6. *Simple to complex.*

Placing simple learning tasks at the beginning of a course and more complex ones towards the end enables the learner to develop his intrinsic sources of motivation. The probability of successfully completing simple tasks is high, and providing a backlog of successful learning will provide psychological support for attempting more complex tasks.

7. *Most to least frequent.*

Learning tasks that will be used most frequently under actual performance conditions should be taught first, with the less frequently used following later in the course.

Guidelines for the arrangement of learning tasks:
1. *General to specific*
2. *Concrete to abstract*
3. *Familiar to unknown*
4. *Scatter interesting tasks*
5. *Logical order*
6. *Simple to complex*
7. *Most to least frequent*

The identification of learning tasks shows the instructor what to teach, while the arrangement indicates to the instructor the order in which they should be taught. Assessment of the learners at the beginning of the course shows where each person should begin in the instructional programme. The identification and arrangement of the learning tasks coupled with the assessment of learners points out the route that each learner must follow in order to achieve the behavioural objectives.

INSTRUCTIONAL PROCESSES

The selection of instructional processes in course planning involves determining how each learning task will be handled. The concern at this stage is with selecting the techniques and instructional aids or devices that appear to have the best potential for assisting learners to achieve the behavioural objectives. The actual use of the instructional processes chosen will be discussed in detail in chapter four, but the selection of the most suitable alternatives is an integral part of course planning and is dealt with here.

The most important consideration in selecting instructional processes is that the factors affecting adult learning be taken into account. In general, the instructor should select instructional processes that:

1. Help the learner establish meaningfulness in new material, either as a pattern or in relation to his previous experience.

2. Provide opportunities for the learner to practice the behaviours that he is to learn.

3. Encourage the immediate application of new material in a practical way.

4. Provide for reinforcement of new behaviours.

5. Give the learner immediate knowledge of results.

6. Provide for active participation by the learners.

7. Help to establish an atmosphere or climate where change is not only possible but actively encouraged.

Factors other than the adult learning process influence the choice of instructional techniques. Some techniques are more suitable than others for behavioural objectives in different domains of learning. Discussion is more effective than the lecture technique for material in the affective domain, while demonstration is more effective than either the lecture or discussion for learning psychomotor skills. Demonstration, however, would rarely be selected as the most effective technique for learning tasks in the cognitive domain.

The characteristics, experience, and abilities of the instructor and the learners influence the selection of techniques and devices. Inexperienced learners or people with a low level of education have difficulty in learning from a lecture. If the learners have not participated in group discussions in the past, they must first learn how that technique functions before they can use it effectively. An inexperienced instructor often has knowledge of and ability with a very limited range of instructional processes, so that he is unable or unwilling to try out new and different techniques. In such cases the instructor frequently decides that the least threatening thing for him to do is to talk, so the lecture technique tends to dominate all of his instruction regardless of the behavioural objectives for the course.

Physical conditions and administrative factors may also influence the choice of instructional processes. It is difficult to conduct group discussions in rooms with fixed seating, and it would be hard to lecture in situations where noisy machinery was in operation. The duration of classroom sessions and lack of access to necessary rooms and equipment may prohibit the use of the most effective instructional processes for specific learning tasks.

Factors affecting the choice of instructional processes:
1. *How adults learn*
2. *Domain of learning*
3. *Nature of the learners*
4. *Abilities of the instructor*
5. *Physical conditions*

The instructional processes that are selected should be carefully chosen for specific learning tasks, and more than one technique should be used. An entire course taught by one technique would be boring to the learners as well as ineffective. A variety of instructional processes should be used in each session of a course. In general, at least three different techniques should be included in each session and the technique should be changed every twenty to thirty minutes, if not oftener.

EVALUATION PROCEDURES

Evaluation procedures are used to determine the effectiveness of instruction in producing the desired changes in the learners. Evaluation is necessary in order to justify the existence of a course, to judge its effectiveness, and to improve the instruction provided to adult learners. Unfortunately, relatively few courses are evaluated with any degree of thoroughness, so it is difficult to determine which courses are effective and which are ineffective. Specific methods and procedures for evaluation are discussed in chapter five, although some decisions about how, what, and when to evaluate must be made during the course-planning process.

The evaluation of adult-education courses is a continuous process, beginning before a course commences and ending after a course is completed. There are five basic elements in a comprehensive evaluation plan for an adult-education course.

1. *Formative course evaluation.*
Formative course evaluation takes place while a course is still in the developmental stage and is used to modify a course before it is given on a full-scale basis. The course may be tried out with a small group of learners or with experts in the field and adjusted as a result of this experience.

2. *Entry-behaviour assessment.*
The entry behaviour of the learners should be assessed either before they come to the course or at the first session. This procedure enables the instructor to determine how the learners stand in relation to the behavioural objectives and learning tasks, and indicates to him the appropriate point at which to begin instruction.

3. *In-progress measurement.*
Various types of tests and ratings are made while the course is in progress so that both the learners and the instructor can assess the rate of progress towards the behavioural objectives. Instruction may then be modified to ensure the optimum attainment of objectives and to provide remedial assistance where needed.

4. *Terminal assessment.*
Terminal assessment is conducted at the conclusion of a

course to ascertain its effectiveness. A wide variety of measurements is usually sought at this stage since it is the final opportunity to observe the learners in the formal instructional setting.

5. *Follow-up.*
Some type of follow-up should be conducted whenever possible to determine whether or not the material learned in the course is being used in the natural societal setting. The course would be judged as ineffective if none of the behaviours were adopted and used by the participants. The follow-up stage should result in some modifications in the course plan to strengthen the relationship between instruction and performance in the natural societal setting.

Elements in a comprehensive evaluation:
1. *Formative course evaluation*
2. *Entry-behaviour assessment*
3. *In-progress measurement*
4. *Terminal assessment*
5. *Follow-up*

The specific types of evaluation to be conducted are closely linked to the behavioural objectives of a course. A properly stated behavioural objective used in course planning indicates the product or behaviour that will be observed, the conditions under which the behaviour must occur, and the standard of performance required. The basic decisions about evaluation are therefore included in the behavioural objectives and it is a relatively simple matter to include and translate those decisions into an evaluation procedure.

CHAPTER THREE POST-ASSESSMENT

When you have read chapter three, complete the post-assessment shown below. Indicate whether each statement is true or false, and the degree of confidence in your answer.

Correctness of Statement	Degree of Confidence
T The statement is true.	1 I guessed at the answer.
F The statement is false.	2 My answer may be correct.
	3 I'm confident that my answer is correct.

1. Behavioural objectives are broad statements of what the instructor expects to accomplish.   T F 1 2 3
2. As long as the instructor knows the objectives of a course, it makes no difference whether or not the learners know them.   T F 1 2 3
3. The objectives of a course should be stated in terms of the terminal behaviour of the participants.   T F 1 2 3
4. An objective describes a pattern of behaviour that the learner is expected to demonstrate at the end of a course.   T F 1 2 3
5. The following objective is expressed in behavioural terms: "The learner will gain a working knowledge of the R.C.A. tape recorder."   T F 1 2 3
6. The following objective is non-behavioural: "The learner will become familiar with the background of World War II."   T F 1 2 3
7. Learning tasks are derived mainly from the goals of a course.   T F 1 2 3
8. Behavioural objectives in the affective domain are the most difficult to write.   T F 1 2 3
9. Behavioural objectives in the cognitive domain are the easiest to write.   T F 1 2 3
10. The learning domain of the behavioural objective should not influence the selection of instructional processes.   T F 1 2 3

The correct answers are given on the next page.

ANSWERS

1. F; 2. F; 3. T; 4. T; 5. F; 6. T; 7. F; 8. T; 9. F; 10. F

If you answered less than 8 items correctly, re-read chapter three carefully, looking for applications of the material.

FOR FURTHER STUDY

1. Kibler, Robert J., Larry L. Barker and David T. Miles. *Behavioral Objectives and Instruction.* Boston: Allyn and Bacon, 1970. (paperback)

2. Mager, Robert F. *Preparing Instructional Objectives.* Palo Alto, California: Fearon Publishers, 1962. (paperback)

3. Mager, Robert F. and Kenneth M. Beach. *Developing Vocational Instruction.* Palo Alto, California: Fearon Publishers, 1967. (paperback)

4

INSTRUCTION: PRE-ASSESSMENT

Before reading chapter four, complete the pre-assessment test given below. Indicate whether the statements are true or false and the degree of confidence in your answer.

Correctness of Statement
T The statement is true.
F The statement is false.

Degree of Confidence
1 I guessed at the answer.
2 My answer may be correct.
3 I'm confident that my answer is correct.

1.	Effective course planning requires that the appropriate instructional techniques be selected before the behavioural objectives are set.	T	F	1	2	3
2.	Group discussion is an effective way of acquiring information.	T	F	1	2	3
3.	Methods of adult education are ways of organizing people for purposes of learning.	T	F	1	2	3
4.	Correspondence study is a technique of adult education.	T	F	1	2	3
5.	Instructional devices can't teach by themselves.	T	F	1	2	3
6.	Group discussion is useful for changing social behaviour.	T	F	1	2	3
7.	Films may be classified as environmental devices.	T	F	1	2	3
8.	A lecture should last for no more than thirty minutes.	T	F	1	2	3
9.	The instructor controls most aspects of instruction in a closed instructional strategy.	T	F	1	2	3
10.	The first component in an instructional sequence is the presentation of new material.	T	F	1	2	3

Please turn to the next page for the correct answers and score your chapter four pre-assessment.

64

ANSWERS

1. F; 2. F; 3. T; 4. F; 5. T; 6. T; 7. F; 8. T; 9. T; 10. F

If you had 9 or 10 correct answers and confidence levels of 2 and 3, skim read chapter four. If you had 7 or 8 correct answers and confidence levels of 1, 2, and 3, read the chapter carefully. If you had 6 or less correct answers and confidence levels of 1 and 2, study the chapter in detail and try to apply the material to your own instructing.

instruction

Instruction is concerned with all of the events in the formal instructional setting that are external to the learner. An instructor is responsible for arranging and controlling the activities of the learner in the way that will most likely result in learning, although there can be no guarantee that learning will occur. The basic decisions about how learning may best be aided are made during the course-planning process, and those decisions are transferred into action when instruction begins.

There is a wide variety of options for the beginning instructor to choose from in developing his own approach to instruction. The instructor must be able to adapt his activities to the particular group he is working with and to the behavioural objectives represented in different courses. To develop this flexibility, the instructor should first know about and understand the general nature of instruction and then be able to select and use the most appropriate instructional strategy for a given course.

COMPONENTS OF INSTRUCTION

Certain elements are common to every instructional situation, and each should be present if learning is to be guided effectively. Robert Gagné, who identified the nine components listed below, suggests that the sequence of events does not always occur in the order given. The components are usually put into practice as a series of verbal directions given to the learner by the instructor.

1. *Gaining and controlling attention.*
By means of statements or gestures, the instructor directs the attention of the learner to the material that is to be learned.
2. *Informing the learner of expected outcomes.*
The instructor tells the learner what his performance should be like when learning is completed.

3. *Stimulating recall of relevant prerequisites.*
Before learning new material, verbal directions are given to the learner so that he will recall the material learned previously that is relevant to the new material.

4. *Presenting the new material.*
The instructor presents the new object, skill, or printed material that is to be learned.

5. *Offering guidance for learning.*
The instructor attempts to facilitate the learning process by providing guidance in the form of questions or directions to the learner.

6. *Providing feedback.*
The instructor informs the learner, or structures the situation so that the learner can find out for himself, whether or not his performance is correct.

7. *Appraising performance.*
At the end of a sequence of instruction, the learner is given an opportunity to appraise his performance against an external standard such as a test.

8. *Making provision for transferability.*
The instructor provides a variety of experiences, examples, and problems so that the learner can transfer the material to a variety of different settings.

9. *Ensuring retention.*
The instructor attempts to ensure that new material will be retained by providing the learner with a number of opportunities for practice and by relating it to previously learned material.

Components of instruction:
1. *Gain and control attention.*
2. *Inform learner of expected outcomes.*
3. *Stimulate recall of relevant prerequisites.*
4. *Present new material.*
5. *Offer guidance for learning.*
6. *Provide feedback.*
7. *Appraise performance.*
8. *Provide for transferability.*
9. *Ensure retention.*

In a group of pre-adult learners, almost all of the components of instruction must be provided by the teacher. In an adult group, however, there is a much greater variety of experiences and information so that some instructional activities can be undertaken by the learning group, particularly in the latter components. A group of adult learners can be quite adept at providing feedback, appraising performance, and providing for transferability, and the instructor's function then becomes that of creating a situation in which the learners are able to assume more and more of the components of instruction.

GENERAL INSTRUCTIONAL STRATEGIES

The strategy used by an instructor may vary depending upon the characteristics of the instructor, the nature of the learners and the behavioural objective at a given time, but there are two general types of strategies.

In a *closed* instructional strategy, the instructor is dominant and controls every aspect of the learning situation. The learners assume a relatively passive role, listening to the instructor and following his directions. An *open* instructional strategy gives the learners a more active part in directing their own learning activities, while the instructor's role is concerned more with providing assistance than with giving firm directions. The open and closed general instructional strategies represent the extremes in a range of strategies that are available, and a particular instructor might be at some point between the two.

General instructional strategies:
1. *Closed*
2. *Open*

Some instructors depend entirely upon one general instructional strategy to the exclusion of all others. A person trained or experienced in group work might rely solely on an open strategy, while an instructor with a background in the armed forces or in pre-adult teaching would be more likely to adopt a closed instructional strategy. An instructor should develop an ability to use a variety of instructional strategies and be able to change from one to another depending upon the situation. A closed strategy might be appropriate when training an adult to perform a specific job, but an open strategy would be more suitable for teaching in the liberal arts. Within a particular course, the general instructional strategy should vary for different behavioural objectives. A closed strategy would be more useful for objectives in the psychomotor domain and at the lower levels of the cognitive domain. At the higher levels of the cognitive and at all levels of the affective domain, an open strategy is usually more suitable. Thus, rather than using one general instructional strategy for all situations, an effective instructor changes his strategy as the occasion demands.

The general instructional strategy chosen for a particular situation provides some guidelines to the instructor as to whether he or the learners should take the main responsibility for carrying out the nine components of instruction mentioned earlier. In general, the more open the strategy, the greater the number of components that are performed by the learners; the more closed the instructional strategy, the greater is the role of the instructor. At the closed extreme of the range of strategies, the nine components are all supplied by the instructor.

INSTRUCTIONAL PROCESSES

In order to use a particular instructional strategy effectively, the instructor must select from a wide variety of instructional processes those that he judges to be the most suitable for specific behavioural objectives and learning tasks. Coolie Verner has suggested that distinctions should be made among three different types of instructional processes, each of which is outlined below and then expanded in the following sections. An ability to make these distinctions is of great assistance to the instructor when he is searching for the most appropriate instructional process to use in a specific situation.

1. *Methods.*
Methods are the ways in which an unknown and undefined body of potential participants may be organized for purposes of directed learning. There are *individual methods* such as

correspondence study, directed individual study, apprentice-ship, and programmed instruction, as well as *group methods* such as the class, discussion group, workshop, and seminar. More often than not the method is chosen by the adminis-trator of an adult-education programme and the instructor must work within the method he selects.

2. *Techniques.*

Techniques are the ways in which an instructor establishes a relationship between himself, the learner, and the material to be learned once the method is determined. Techniques may be classified according to their main functions, which include acquiring information (the lecture), applying knowledge (group discussion), and acquiring skills (demonstration).

3. *Devices.*

Devices are instructional aids that increase the effectiveness of techniques but do not teach by themselves. The four main types of instructional devices, and examples of each, are illustrative (films), extension (television), manipulative (tools), and environmental devices (seating arrangements).

Instructional processes:

1. Methods
    a. Individual.
    b. Group.

2. Techniques
    a. For acquiring information.
    b. For applying knowledge.
    c. For acquiring a skill.

3. Devices
    a. Illustrative.
    b. Extension.
    c. Manipulative.
    d. Environmental.

Individual Methods

Individual methods are used when individuals are in isolation and can't be brought together in a learning group or when individualized programmes of study must be prepared for each learner. Thus, the basic element in all individual methods is a one-to-one relationship between the instructor and the learner.

Correspondence study consists of a series of written lessons developing some subject matter through a logical sequence of relatively small steps. The relationship between the learner and instructor is handled through the mail. Correspondence study is one of the more commonly used methods of adult education, and students taking a course by this method usually achieve as high or higher marks than those who attend classes. The drop-out rate in correspondence study is usually much higher than in any other method.

Directed individual study is similar to correspondence study. The main difference between the two methods is that there is some opportunity for direct contact between instructor and learner in directed individual study. In a series of face-to-face meetings, the instructor can direct the learner to various sources of information and plan a sequence of activities for him in much the same manner as occurs in correspondence study. This method is particularly useful with small numbers of students and where there is a wide range of abilities or interests.

Apprenticeship is used extensively in vocational education. The chief feature of the method is that a learner works under the close supervision and direction of one who is expert in the skills to be learned. A similar method is often used in education for the professions, where it is usually called internship.

Programmed instruction is an individual method characterized by an orderly presentation of material in small steps with immediate knowledge of results provided at each step. A good programme is extremely difficult to write as it requires a considerable amount of planning, testing, and revising to ensure that no steps are left out of the sequence. There is a considerable amount of programmed material available from commercial publishers which can be used in conjunction with group methods for special learning problems.

Group Methods

Group methods in adult education are used to instruct a number of learners at one time. They have the advantage of being more economical than individual instruction. In addition, some kinds of learning can occur in a group that would be difficult, if not impossible, to duplicate in an individual setting. A group can be a powerful influence on behaviour, and people can learn about group processes by participating in them.

The *class* is probably the group method that is most familiar to beginning instructors because of their own high-school or university experience. A class may consist of from five to five hundred or more students brought together in one place especially for purposes of learning. Both the time period and duration of the class as well as the general subject-matter area are usually determined in advance. The class is basically a collection of individuals with each person learning on his own. Only occasionally does a class become a real social group in which group processes become a major influence on learning.

The *seminar* method presents an opportunity for group members to do independent research, present their findings to the seminar, and discuss and evaluate the products of research. For these activities to occur effectively, the seminar size is generally about ten to fifteen members. Some features of the seminar method could be adapted and used in another method. For example, individual or small-group projects may be undertaken, researched, presented, and discussed.

The *discussion group* method is more common in liberal adult education than in other types of courses. In this method, the learning group is formed specifically for discussion purposes and rarely involves more than twenty learners. The instructor is usually called a discussion leader or group leader, and he shares with the learners the responsibility for organizing and directing the activities of the discussion group.

In the *workshop* method, a group of people with a common interest or problem gather together under the leadership of one or several experts to explore specific aspects of a topic or to seek solutions to their problems. The workshop may include forty or fifty learners and generally consists of day-long sessions lasting anywhere from one day to three weeks.

> *Methods include:*
> *1. Individual: correspondence study, directed individual study, apprenticeship, programmed instruction.*
> *2. Group: class, discussion group, workshop, seminar.*

Techniques for Acquiring Information

The technique for acquiring information which is used most frequently is the *lecture*. It tends to dominate instruction in the class method, too often to the complete exclusion of other techniques. As a result, the lecture is both overused and misused.

In the pure lecture technique, the instructor presents to the class an oral discourse on a particular subject. This is the extreme form of closed instruction, where the instructor has complete responsibility for the activity and the learner is passive. The size of the class makes relatively little difference when a lecture is presented, so that the lecture can be given by television or tape recording and be just as effective as when given in person.

The research studies that have investigated the effectiveness of the lecture technique indicate that the lecture is suitable for the following purposes:

1. When the instruction is concerned mainly with giving information.
2. When the information to be given isn't readily available somewhere else.
3. When the material must be organized in a special way for a particular group.
4. When establishing learner interest in a subject is one of the objectives.
5. When the material presented is needed only for short-term retention.

6. When introducing a subject or giving oral directions for learning tasks that will involve other techniques.

In other kinds of situations, however, the lecture is not a very useful technique. The lecture should not be used in the following situations:

1. When the instructional objective involves anything other than acquiring information.

2. When the learning task is concerned with changing attitudes, values, or observable behaviours.

3. When the information must be available for long-term retention.

4. When the material is complex, detailed or abstract.

5. When the intelligence or education of the learners is average or less.

6. When participation in the learning activity is an important aspect of the objective.

7. When the material must be analysed or integrated with previously learned material.

If the instructor has considered the guidelines given above and decided that the lecture is the proper technique to use, there are a number of things that can be done to ensure its effectiveness.

1. Don't present too many points. Six major points would probably be enough for a thirty-minute lecture.

2. Summaries should be presented both at the beginning and the end of the lecture. During the lecture, pause occasionally to give the learners a chance to summarize for themselves, and encourage them to do so.

3. The material presented should be made as meaningful as possible to the learners in terms of their previous experience and as a pattern. This could be done through illustrations, charts, and diagrams, and a small amount of chalkboard work.

4. The length of the lecture should not exceed thirty minutes.

5. In making the presentation, the sentences should be short and the language and style kept as simple as possible.

6. The speed of speaking should be adjusted to the complexity of the material and the experience of the learners.

7. The lecture should be improved by using some instructional devices to emphasize important points.

8. Other techniques that provide for learner participation, such as question periods and buzz groups, should be used in conjunction with the lecture.

Most of the other techniques used for acquiring information are merely variations of the lecture. A *panel* consists of several brief lectures given by different people. A panel is useful when there are a number of different views on a subject that must be presented. A *debate* presents a conflict situation, in which opposing sides each present short speeches followed by rebuttals. The same principles of effectiveness that were found in the lecture technique also apply to the panel, debate, and similar techniques.

Field trips are another technique for acquiring information about how particular aspects of a job are performed in a real situation. Thorough briefings are required before the field trip begins so that the learners will be alerted to the kinds of knowledge they are expected to gain, and new learnings should be summarized and discussed immediately after the field trip.

Some techniques for acquiring information: *1. Lecture* *2. Debate* *3. Panel* *4. Field trip*

Techniques for Applying Knowledge

Knowledge may be acquired in a number of different ways, including the use of instructional techniques for acquiring information, reading, project assignments, and work experience. For the knowledge gained to be used effectively, the instructor should provide opportunities in the formal instructional setting for the learner to try out various ways of applying new material.

A *buzz group* consists of four to six people who meet for five to ten minutes to discuss a task assigned by the instructor. The small group forms a circle, which encourages everyone in the group to participate in the discussion. The buzz group does not have a designated leader, although one person may be selected as a recorder or reporter to present the outcomes of the discussion to the larger group. The task assigned to the buzz groups should be quite specific, phrased in terms that are readily understood by the learners, and be capable of completion within the time allotted. The buzz groups might be asked to solve a problem, to decide on one question to ask the instructor, or to review information that has been presented previously. When the buzz groups have completed their task, brief reports may be given to the larger group by the reporter from each small group. The buzz-group technique is a useful way of providing opportunities for full learner participation in a large class, and it is used most frequently in combination with the lecture technique.

The *group-discussion* technique involves a group of from six to twenty learners who discuss a topic with the guidance of a discussion leader—usually the course instructor. In some instances a recorder may be asked to write down information that the group feels may be useful. An observer may be selected to watch the process involved in the discussion and to report back to the group periodically. Thus, the recorder's role is concerned primarily with the content of the discussion, the observer is concerned with the process, and the leader is responsible for co-ordinating the various elements of the group discussion to ensure that the objectives are achieved and that the discussion doesn't break down into an exchange of ignorance or a 'bull session'.

The leader of a group discussion should not assume a dominant role once the discussion is underway. Rather, his principal responsibility is with preparing himself and the participants in advance so that the maximum learning can be achieved. The leader should read information about the topic to be discussed, prepare some relevant questions for the group to discuss, make sure that the physical arrangements are suitable, and introduce the topic to the group. The leader should also attempt to ensure that the participants are briefed adequately as to the content, purpose, and procedures of the group discussion.

Effective use of the group-discussion technique requires that the participants have a background of knowledge in the topic to be discussed, so that each member of the group has the potential to contribute and develop his own applications of the material. A good discussion topic should interest the participants and be clearly worded so that it is readily understood. Participants should possess or be able to acquire enough information about the topic to discuss it meaningfully. A good discussion topic should also suggest the possibility of different points of view.

Once the group discussion begins, the leader tends to move into the background, intervening only when necessary to provide information, clarification, or redirection. The communication pattern of the members may be observed either by the leader or by a participant designated as an observer. In either case, the participation of the group members can be charted using a *sociometric diagram* like the one illustrated in Figure 7. The diagram shows the pattern of interaction in part of a group discussion among six people. The lines and arrows indicate where the statements were directed, while the numbers indicate the order of speaking. Individual A, who was the leader of the group, began by asking a question of the group as a whole. F and E responded to A, who then directed a comment to E. B said nothing during the entire discussion.

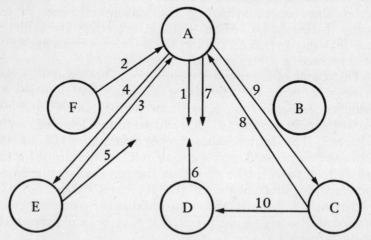

Figure 7. Illustration of a Sociometric Diagram

This kind of sociometric diagram helps the instructor to

understand how the group is functioning, and it is possible to identify the informal 'leaders' as well as the 'isolates' who do not participate actively in the discussion.

The *role-playing* technique provides learners with an opportunity to try out various types of behaviour in a relatively non-threatening atmosphere. The participants can act out situations or problems relevant to the natural societal setting in different ways, select the approaches that seem to be most successful, and then practise them. The main tasks of the instructor are to prepare the learners for role playing and to guide them through the technique.

When the learners have a sufficient background of knowledge that can be used to generate new behaviours, a five-step sequence of events is normally followed in directing the role-playing technique.

1. The idea of role-playing is introduced by describing briefly the purpose for using the technique and the situation and roles that are to be acted out.
2. The members of the group are invited to participate by asking for volunteers.
3. The instructor restates and explains the situation and roles in greater detail and tells the group what to watch for.
4. The situation is acted out by the persons who have taken the roles.
5. The group is given an opportunity to assess the behaviours of the role players through analysis and discussion, and ideas for different behaviours are tried out.

Varying degrees of preparation are possible when role playing is used. In some cases the behaviours should be planned in detail and the actors thoroughly prepared, while in other situations only a brief description is necessary. The instructor may play one of the roles himself if there is a specific type of behaviour he wishes to demonstrate. Role playing should not be used when time is short, nor should an instructor attempt to use the technique to provide therapy for group members.

> *Some techniques for applying knowledge:*
> *1. Buzz groups*
> *2. Group discussion*
> *3. Role playing*

Techniques for Acquiring a Skill

The final category of instructional techniques consists of those used for acquiring a skill, which is the principal goal of many vocational adult education courses. In addition to the principles of learning presented in chapter one, there are several other factors involved in learning a skill. Every effort should be made to ensure that the skill becomes automatic, so that the learner doesn't have to review mentally the operation each time he performs it. In addition, the skill should be learned and practised under conditions that are as similar as possible to those in the natural societal setting, so that the learner will have minimum difficulty in transferring the skill from the formal instructional setting.

A useful way of thinking about skill learning is the *Horizon of Minimal Learning* shown in Figure 8. The H.O.M.L. is the point at which the skill can be performed satisfactorily. If the skill is practised only until the H.O.M.L. is reached, as shown in situation A, then the customary loss following learning will leave performance at an inadequate level. If the skill is practised beyond the H.O.M.L., as shown in situation B, the expected loss will still result in adequate performance. This concept is sometimes referred to as *overlearning*.

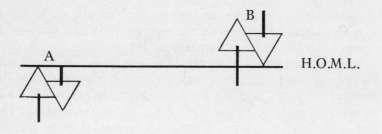

Figure 8. Horizon of Minimal Learning

Herbert J. Klausmeier lists seven principles which apply to all skill learning. Those principles are summarized below.

1. Analyse the skill in detail before attempting to guide the learner.
2. Demonstrate the correct response for the learner.

3. Guide the learner's first tries verbally and, if necessary, guide them physically also.

4. Provide for appropriate practice tasks.

5. Use distributed rather than massed practice.

6. Provide the learner with knowledge of results and correct any inadequate responses.

7. Help the learner to evaluate his own responses.

The basic techniques used in acquiring a skill are the process demonstration and practice. In the *process demonstration,* the instructor shows how something is done and explains it step by step while the learners watch and listen. This is done so that the learners will understand a procedure before trying to follow it themselves. The demonstration is usually followed by *practice*, where the learners perform the activity under the guidance of the instructor. The process-demonstration and practice sequence usually follows the steps listed below.

1. Explain the purpose and objectives of the demonstration.

2. Review any previous material that is relevant to the demonstration.

3. Arrange the group around the instructor so that everyone has a clear view.

4. Outline briefly the operation you are about to perform so that the learners will know what to look for.

5. Perform the demonstration fairly quickly using a simple oral description of what you are doing.

6. Repeat the demonstration more slowly, emphasizing the key points.

7. Answer any questions, summarize the demonstration, and hand out prepared notes if necessary.

8. Have several students give a 'return demonstration' to see whether or not any key points are being overlooked.

9. If there is sufficient equipment, have all the learners practise the operation together at the same time.

10. Have the learners practise individually and correct any errors immediately so that the incorrect method is not learned.

> *The principal techniques for acquiring a skill are:*
> 1. *Process demonstration.*
> 2. *Practice.*

Devices

The term *devices* refers to a wide variety of instructional aids that increase the effectiveness of instruction but that do not teach by themselves. Devices must be chosen carefully by the instructor for specific purposes and must be used in conjunction with instructional techniques in order to increase their effectiveness.

Instructional devices are often both overused and misused. Instructors sometimes assume that, because a device such as a film is readily available, it is the best way of teaching a particular topic. This is not necessarily the case. Every device should be previewed and evaluated in terms of whether or not it is appropriate for specific behavioural objectives. If it passes that evaluation, the device should be integrated into the course at the most suitable moment.

Illustrative devices include such items as photographs, posters, slides, motion pictures, film loops, and the chalkboard. These devices are used in conjunction with a number of instructional techniques such as the lecture and process demonstration in order to establish meaningfulness and to provide additional exposure to certain key points.

Extension devices such as radio and television are used to extend an instructional technique such as the lecture to more people than could be contacted directly. In most cases the listeners or viewers are not in a formal instructional setting, so it is difficult to observe and guide their learning directly. The effectiveness of extension devices can be improved by forming listening groups to discuss a broadcast.

Manipulative devices are the tools or equipment necessary in learning a skill. The instructor should attempt to provide manipulative devices that are suitable to the physiological characteristics of each learner.

Environmental devices are factors in the instructional setting that have the potential to affect learning. The temperature and ventilation of the room, the adequacy of lighting, and the seating arrangements are all included in this category of devices. The seating arrangements should be altered to suit the technique being used and the preferences of the group. Adults tend to dislike sitting in straight rows of chairs, and that type of seating arrangement would be entirely inappropriate for conducting a group discussion. A circular, semi-circular, or horseshoe arrangement of seats enables the learners to see each other and encourages participation. No seating arrangement should be considered permanent.

> *Types of instructional devices:*
> 1. *Illustrative*
> 2. *Extension*
> 3. *Manipulative*
> 4. *Environmental*

A FINAL WORD

The instructional processes discussed in this chapter are by no means the only ones that an instructor can use. There are dozens of methods, techniques, and devices, but the ones presented here constitute the basic processes that are used most frequently. The creative instructor can improvise on these basic patterns until he masters a variety of processes. Then he will be able to adapt quickly to the needs of a particular group and the behavioural objectives of a specific course.

CHAPTER FOUR POST-ASSESSMENT

When you have read chapter four, complete the post-assessment shown below. Indicate whether each statement is true or false and show the degree of confidence in your answer.

Correctness of Statement
T The statement is true.
F The statement is false.

Degree of Confidence
1 I guessed at the answer.
2 My answer may be correct.
3 I'm confident that my answer is correct.

1. It is not necessary to change the instructional technique periodically if group processes are used.	T F 1 2 3
2. The lecture is an effective way of learning how to apply knowledge.	T F 1 2 3
3. The process demonstration is a method of adult education.	T F 1 2 3
4. Techniques of adult education are ways of helping specific groups of adults to learn.	T F 1 2 3
5. Instructional devices may be used as a substitute for an instructor.	T F 1 2 3
6. The lecture is an effective way of changing social behaviour.	T F 1 2 3
7. The chalkboard may be classified as an illustrative device.	T F 1 2 3
8. A lecture should not present material that is needed for long-term retention.	T F 1 2 3
9. The final component in an instructional sequence is the provision of feedback.	T F 1 2 3
10. The learner controls most aspects of instruction in an open instructional strategy.	T F 1 2 3

The correct answers are given on the next page.

ANSWERS

1. F; 2. F; 3. F; 4. T; 5. F; 6. F; 7. T; 8. T; 9. F; 10. T

If you answered less than 8 items correctly, re-read chapter four carefully and try to apply the material to your own situation.

FOR FURTHER STUDY

1. Leypoldt, Martha M. *40 Ways To Teach in Groups.* Valley Forge: Judson Press, 1967. (paperback)

2. Miller, Harry L. *Teaching and Learning in Adult Education.* New York: Macmillan, 1964.

3. Verner, Coolie, and Alan Booth. *Adult Education.* New York: Center for Applied Research in Education, 1964.

5

EVALUATION: PRE-ASSESSMENT

Before reading chapter five, complete the pre-assessment test given below. Indicate whether the statements are true or false and the degree of confidence in your answer.

Correctness of Statement	Degree of Confidence
T The statement is true.	1 I guessed at the answer.
F The statement is false.	2 My answer may be correct.
	3 I'm confident that my answer is correct.

1. Objectives are useful in course planning, but they play a secondary role in the evaluation process.   T F 1 2 3

2. A content test measures a learner product under artificial conditions.   T F 1 2 3

3. The second component of an instructional model is pre-assessment of the learners.   T F 1 2 3

4. Evaluation is used primarily to assess the success of the learners, not the success of instruction.   T F 1 2 3

5. Criterion-referenced tests are more useful in adult education than are norm-referenced tests.   T F 1 2 3

6. Terminal evaluation is used to help determine the effectiveness of an educational programme while it is in the developmental stage.   T F 1 2 3

7. Criterion-referenced tests are used to establish a learner's status with respect to other adults.   T F 1 2 3

8. A pre-test is used to determine the status of the learner in relation to the objectives of the course.   T F 1 2 3

9. Evaluating learner performance under artificial conditions is referred to as a non-reactive measurement.   T F 1 2 3

10. Test items used to measure recall memory are easy to score but hard to construct.   T F 1 2 3

Please turn the page for the correct answers and score your chapter five pre-assessment.

ANSWERS

1. F; 2. T; 3. T; 4. F; 5. T; 6. F; 7. F; 8. T; 9. F; 10. F

If you had 9 or 10 correct answers and confidence levels of 2 and 3, skim read chapter five. If you had 7 or 8 correct answers and confidence levels of 1, 2, and 3, read the chapter carefully. If you had 6 or less correct answers and confidence levels of 1 and 2, study the chapter in detail and try to apply the material to your own instructing.

evaluation

Several factors have contributed to a persistent lack of evaluation of adult-education courses and programmes. Many adult-education activities are offered once and never repeated, so that a thorough evaluation is seen to be too time-consuming and expensive in relation to the potential benefit that could be derived. Some instructors hesitate to evaluate, either out of fear of the results or because they don't feel they are competent to conduct an evaluation. In fact, designing a comprehensive and useful evaluation programme is a complex process requiring considerable knowledge and skill, but the part-time instructor can obtain much helpful information from evaluation if he is willing to take the time and make the effort required.

The evaluation process determines to what extent the learning experiences that are designed and applied by the instructor are actually producing the desired changes in learner behaviour. The information collected in evaluation is used to judge the appropriateness and effectiveness of instruction, to modify and improve the course, to make decisions about the further learning needs of adults, and to guide administrative decisions about the practicality of courses and the effectiveness of instructors.

SYSTEMATIC EVALUATION

The importance of evaluation in adult education comes into focus quite clearly with the aid of an instructional model shown in Figure 9. After the behavioural objectives have been specified, the learners are assessed before any instruction is given to determine how they stand in relation to the course objectives. This step enables the instructor to adapt his procedures and material to the general level of the group and to the specific needs of individual learners. When instruction has been completed, a post-assessment is carried out, again to determine how the learners stand in relation to the behavioural objectives for the course.

The post-assessment provides the instructor with information that enables him to judge how effective his instruction has been. If all or most of the learners appear to have attained the behavioural objectives, they might be augmented the next time that the course is presented. If a considerable number of learners have not attained the objectives, then the problem may lie either with the objectives or with the instruction that was given. The instructor should therefore consider revising the objectives to reflect more realistically the nature of the adults who take the course. He should also consider revising the instructional procedures so that they will be more effective in helping adults learn.

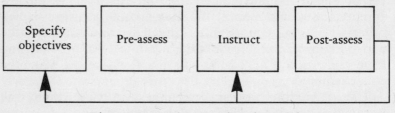

Figure 9. An Instructional Model

The instructional model emphasizes two major types of evaluation that are closely linked to instruction, but a complete evaluation schedule should begin well before a course starts and continue after the course is completed. The five types of evaluation that should be included were mentioned briefly in chapter three and are expanded upon in greater detail in the following paragraphs. In the order in which they are conducted, the types of evaluation are formative course evaluation, entry-behaviour assessment, in-progress measurement, terminal assessment, and follow-up.

Formative Course Evaluation

Formative course evaluation provides some initial information as to the suitability of the course that is being planned while it is still in the developmental stage and relatively easy to alter. The course plan may first be presented to a number of experts or to persons working in the field to obtain their critical comments. The course may then be given either as a whole or in part to a small number of adults similar to those who would eventually participate in it. This field test of the course assists the instructor in setting and revising the behavioural objectives, determining whether or not sufficient and appropriate learning tasks are included, and in judging the suitability of the instructional processes that will be used. Thus, the information obtained in formative course evaluation permits the instructor to avoid some deficiencies in the course plan that might otherwise escape detection until a larger group of learners was finding difficulty with the actual course.

A course should be able to satisfy three main criteria of suitability when the formative evaluation is completed. If the course seems designed to enable the learners to attain the behavioural objectives in the time allotted, it meets the criterion of *effectiveness.* When the objectives, learning tasks, and instructional objectives are consistent with the performance analysis and appear to suit the needs of the potential participants, the course meets the criterion of *appropriateness.* The final criterion, *practicality*, is satisfied if the course will not be too difficult or expensive to conduct.

> *Main criteria for course suitability:*
> 1. *Effectiveness.*
> 2. *Appropriateness.*
> 3. *Practicality.*

Entry-Behaviour Assessment

When he first meets the group of adults who will be taking his course, the instructor should assess their entry behaviour in relation to the behavioural objectives for the course. This pre-assessment establishes a base-line of knowledge, skills, and attitudes of the learners when they begin the course. The instructor will then take similar measurements at the end of the course to determine what changes have occurred.

In some instances, the entry-behaviour assessment will establish that the participants are at similar stages in the learning process, in which case instruction can begin with various kinds of group activities. In the majority of courses, however, the pre-assessment procedures will determine that the learners come with a wide variety of entry behaviours.

This indicates a need for individualized forms of instruction to be provided from the start. Some participants may already have attained some of the behavioural objectives, so that additional instruction in those areas would be pointless. Others may be so deficient in their range of existing behaviours that they would have no chance of attaining the behavioural objectives, and those learners would require special assistance on a modified instructional programme.

In-Progress Measurement

In-progress measurements are made at frequent intervals during the course to determine how the learners are progressing in attaining the behavioural objectives. The measuring instruments used are similar to those employed in entry-behaviour assessment since both types of evaluation are related to the course objectives. The results obtained by in-progress measurement are used to modify instruction, to diagnose areas where learners are having difficulty, and to provide knowledge of results to the learners.

In-progress measurements should be informal and brief, and the results should be made known to the learners as quickly as possible so that they can evaluate their own progress. Delaying knowledge of results for even a few days is not as effective in helping adults to learn as is immediate feedback about learning progress. Both the learners and the instructor can use the results of in-progress measurement to adjust their strategies for subsequent parts of the course. The instructor can provide additional assistance or a different form of instruction where progress is not sufficient, and he can use those who have attained the objectives to assist those who have not. On their part, the learners may decide to do extra reading assignments, more studying, or take on other activities after they discover their progress to date. They may even decide to quit the course if they sense that there is little prospect of attaining the objectives or, conversely, that they have little to gain from continuing.

Other forms of in-progress measurement may be used by the instructor in addition to paper-and-pencil tests. Frequent tardiness and absenteeism, for example, are indicators of a lack of interest in the course, while remaining after a session or borrowing books on the subject can be indications that interest is high. The instructor may observe the participation of the learners in group discussions or note the questions that are asked by a student as a rough measure of learning progress. The experienced instructor trains himself to be alert to a variety of cues from the participants which help him to determine how they are progressing in the course.

Terminal Assessment

Terminal assessment, which is sometimes referred to as summative evaluation, is conducted at the conclusion of a course and is the final opportunity for the instructor to observe learner performance in the formal instructional setting. In many courses, terminal assessment is the only form of evaluation that is used. Unfortunately, terminal assessment in itself does not indicate what the participants have learned during the course, nor does it give the instructor a measure of how successful the instruction has been. The participants may already have possessed most of the behaviours or material that was taught, or they may have learned them in other ways outside of the formal instructional setting. Without a pre-assessment of entry behaviour, the instructor can't establish any relationship between the instruction provided and the terminal behaviour of the participants.

Various measures of participant satisfaction are used frequently in short-term adult-education activities. Several questions are usually asked, such as "What did you like most about the programme?" "What did you like least about the programme?" and "How do you think the programme could have been improved?" The replies that the participants give to those and similar questions provide some information about attitudes toward the programme, but satisfaction is not necessarily an indication of learning.

The main usefulness of terminal evaluation is to provide information for the modification of the course for future participants. There is usually no further opportunity for the instructor to provide additional or remedial instruction to the learning group that was evaluated.

92

Follow-Up

The instructor should attempt to follow up his former students whenever possible to determine the degree to which learning in the formal instructional setting is applied or transferred to the natural societal setting. The higher the amount of transfer, the more suitable is the course for the particular group for which it was designed. Former students should be able to make valuable comments that will assist the instructor in improving the course.

On a relatively informal basis, the instructor can determine how many of the behaviours that were included in the course were applied in the natural societal setting. There has been a considerable amount of research, especially in the field of agricultural extension, as to how new ideas and practices are adopted. The *adoption process,* or the mental stages through which an individual passes from the time he first hears about a new behaviour until he uses it all the time, consists of the five elements outlined below.

1. *Awareness.* The individual is exposed to a new behaviour but lacks complete information about it and is not motivated to seek further information.
2. *Interest.* The individual becomes interested in a new behaviour and purposely seeks more information about it.
3. *Evaluation.* The individual mentally applies the new behaviour to his current and anticipated future situation and decides whether or not to try it.
4. *Trial.* The individual uses the new behaviour on a limited scale to determine its usefulness to him.
5. *Adoption.* The individual decides to make full use of the new behaviour in every appropriate situation.

The formal instructional setting can guide a person to the third stage, evaluation, but subsequent stages must be carried out in the natural societal setting in most cases. The follow-up process will enable the instructor to ascertain whether or not the course results in participants moving to the trial and adoption stages, and may suggest modifications to the course so that the learners will be more likely to adopt the behaviours learned in the formal instructional setting. The measurement of behavioural change by adoption is the most powerful evidence that an instructor could obtain about the effectiveness of his instruction.

> *In summary, the five major types of evaluation are:*
> *1. Formative course evaluation.*
> *2. Entry-behaviour assessment.*
> *3. In-progress measurement.*
> *4. Terminal assessment.*
> *5. Follow-up.*

BEHAVIOURAL OBJECTIVES AND EVALUATION

The planning objectives prepared for a course determine the type of evaluation that will be conducted. As discussed in chapter three, the elements of a planning objective include the behaviours that are sought, the conditions under which the behaviour is to be demonstrated, and the standard of performance required. The planning objectives are translated into evaluation devices that measure whether or not the behavioural objective has been attained by the learner.

There is an important difference between evaluation of instruction based upon behavioural objectives, and evaluation of instruction planned on the basis of subject matter or teacher activities. When instruction is centred on content material or instructor activities, *norm-referenced* measurements are used in order to rank students in terms of their ability. The measures used must differentiate among the learners so that a wide range of scores can be obtained. The participants are then assigned a letter grade or percentage mark relative to their position in the group. When instruction is based on behavioural objectives, however, *criterion-referenced* measurements are used. The purpose of criterion-referenced measurement is to determine whether or not each learner has attained the behavioural objective.

> *Types of measurement:*
> *1. Criterion-referenced*
> *2. Norm-referenced*

There is a tendency to rely upon paper-and-pencil tests when evaluating the attainment of behavioural objectives; however, the content test represents only one of four general categories of indices for observing behavioural change. The content test is an index of a learner product obtained under conditions that are created artificially by an instructor. In addition to the learner product under artificial conditions, the instructor may also observe a learner product under natural conditions and learner performance under both artificial and natural conditions. Those four types of indices for assessing the attainment of behavioural objectives are explained below with examples.

1. *Learner product, artificial conditions.*
The content test is the most frequently used index in this category. The instructor creates a situation in which the learner must respond in a pre-determined way. The product of the learner's response is a completed test which is scored by the instructor. Other indices in this category include written essays, completed assignments, and attitude scales.

2. *Learner product, natural conditions.*
The instructor occasionally has an opportunity to observe learner products under natural conditions where the instructor does not create a situation in order to bring about a particular response. An unsolicited letter expressing a favourable attitude about a course, or an opportunity to observe an item produced by a student in his home workshop, are illustrations of indices in this category.

3. *Learner performance, artificial conditions.*
The instructor makes frequent observations of learner performance in the formal instructional setting, especially when skills are being learned and practised. To obtain such measures, the instructor sets a task for the learners to perform while he observes the procedures that they follow. The observations may be recorded on a performance-rating scale or a checklist.

4. *Learner performance, natural conditions.*
Examples of behavioural indices in this category include borrowing extra library books, registration in related courses, and instructor observations of learner activities during rest periods and coffee breaks. The instructor makes no attempt to direct such behaviours, so they reflect fairly well the actual attitudes or performance of the learners.

> *Categories of behavioural indices:*
> 1. *Product under artificial conditions.*
> 2. *Product under natural conditions.*
> 3. *Performance under artificial conditions.*
> 4. *Performance under natural conditions.*

The general advantage of observations made under natural conditions is that they are *non-reactive*. In other words, the method used does not influence the behaviour of the learner or the results obtained from the measuring process. Measurements made under artificial conditions are *reactive* because the method of making the observations does affect the results obtained. An attitude scale, for example, may create rather than measure attitudes, whereas noting the number of library books borrowed is an indirect measure of an attitude which does not affect the behaviour of the learner.

EVALUATION AND LEARNING DOMAINS

The many different kinds of things that an adult can learn in a formal instructional setting were noted and classified in ·chapter one. A course may have behavioural objectives related to three general areas or domains of learning: the cognitive, the affective, and the psychomotor. Since learning may occur in each domain and behavioural objectives may be set for each domain, the instructor should attempt to find a suitable way of evaluating the changes that occur in each domain of learning. That task requires a variety of measurement devices. *Content tests* are the chief method of measuring learning in the cognitive domain; *attitude scales* are used frequently to measure changes in the affective domain; and *rating scales* are used to measure psychomotor learning. Those measuring devices are discussed briefly in the following paragraphs, and principles for constructing the evaluation instruments are presented in the subsequent section.

Content tests usually measure either recall, recognition, or a combination of the two types of memory. Tests measuring recall use essay, short-answer, and sentence-completion items. These are sometimes called *subjective* tests because a variety of answers is possible and the judgement of the instructor determines the score given. An essay may be given a grade of 40 by one instructor, while the same essay might be scored as 80 by another instructor. The main advantage of subjective test items is that they give the learner a chance to organize and present material in a unique form which is the type of behaviour sought at the higher levels of the cognitive domain. Tests measuring recognition use items like true-false questions, multiple choice, or matching items from one column with those in another column. Such tests are sometimes called *objective* because only one answer is correct and the judgement of the instructor doesn't influence the scores obtained. Objective tests are easy to score but very difficult to construct properly, and the items generally measure learning in the lower levels of the cognitive domain.

Attitude scales that accurately measure learning in the affective domain are extremely difficult to construct. Because of this, the instructor should be concerned chiefly with measuring general tendencies rather than making fine distinctions. Determining whether an attitude is positive or negative, favourable or unfavourable, will be sufficient information for the instructor's purposes in most cases. It is fairly easy for a learner to falsify an attitude by the responses that he makes on an attitude scale, so the instructor should also observe the kinds of learner behaviour that reflect a learner's attitudes. The usefulness of an attitude scale can be increased if a high level of trust is established between the instructor and the participants in a course.

Rating scales are used for evaluating learner products or performance in the psychomotor domain. Rating may be done on a relative or absolute basis. *Relative* rating compares several people in a group by assigning each person a rank (first, second, third) or by comparing each person with each other person. *Absolute* rating assigns a score independently of other scores. There are several methods of doing this. A numerical scale consisting of 5 to 9 points, or a descriptive scale such as poor-fair-good-excellent-superior, may be used. For learning certain kinds of procedures a checklist is useful where each item on the list is checked off as it is performed correctly. A product scale is another method of absolute rating, in which the product made by the learner is compared against a scale showing various degrees of perfection. If the learner's product is similar to a poor one, then he can easily see that his performance needs improvement.

> *Learning domains and evaluative instruments:*
> *1. Cognitive domain—content tests*
> *2. Affective domain—attitude scales*
> *3. Psychomotor domain—rating scales*

The principal requirement of the measuring devices used in every domain of learning is that they have *content validity*. This means that an instrument must measure exactly what it is supposed to measure and nothing else. The items used for evaluative purposes must measure the specific type of learning required by the behavioural objective, and should not test related behaviours. Thus, if a content test is used in an attempt to measure cognitive learning at the higher levels, true-false or multiple-choice items would not normally be included as they are not valid measures of the behavioural objective. Similarly, a content test which measures learning in the cognitive domain would not be a valid measure of psychomotor learning. In selecting or developing evaluation instruments with content validity, the instructor must first note the learning domain involved and then consider the specific type of behaviour required by the learner.

CONSTRUCTING EVALUATION INSTRUMENTS

The detailed requirements of constructing and assessing formal evaluation instruments are beyond the scope of this book; however, some general guidelines for preparing tests and scales for use in the typical adult-education programme are suggested in the following pages. The instruments used for evaluation should possess four characteristics:

1. *Validity*. In addition to content validity, which was discussed previously, the measuring devices used with adult learners should be related to subsequent performance in the natural societal setting. Individuals who perform well on the evaluation instrument should do well on similar tasks in everyday life, while those who do poorly in one situation should do poorly in the other.

2. *Reliability*. An evaluation instrument should yield con-

sistent results. If it is used several times with different groups and produces similar results each time, then the instrument is said to be reliable.

3. *Objectivity.* The results obtained by using an objective measuring instrument are not influenced by the person who administers the device and interprets the learner responses. The items in the evaluation instrument should therefore lead to concrete, observable learner products.

4. *Practicality.* The evaluation instrument must conform to practical considerations of cost, time, and convenience. The instructor should assess the practicality of every measuring device in view of the potential benefits that would be derived from its use. In general, the simpler the instrument, the more practical it is to use.

Requirements of evaluation instruments:
1. *Validity*
2. *Reliability*
3. *Objectivity*
4. *Practicality*

Content Tests

There are several types of content-test items that can be used, and a test may contain several different types of items. The chief concern in constructing content-test items is that they attempt to measure the behaviour specified by the course objectives.

True-false content-test items are one type of *dichotomous* question where the respondent must choose between two alternatives. He may be asked to indicate whether a statement is true or false, respond with a yes or no, agree or disagree, or approve or disapprove. Since this type of item provides only two choices, the statements should be clearly either correct or incorrect without additional qualifications. Each item should be restricted to one central idea. Words like 'always', 'none', 'may', and 'frequently' should be avoided as they can suggest the preferred response even if the learner doesn't know the answer. There should be a balance between the number of statements that are true and false, and they should be mixed randomly so that there is no pattern for the respondent to detect.

Multiple-choice items consist of a direct question or an incomplete statement followed by several alternative answers. The question or statement is known as the stem of the item, and the three or four incorrect answers are referred to as distractors. All of the distractors should be equally plausible to those who do not know the correct answer. As much of the item as possible should be included in the stem, and the alternative responses should be consistent grammatically.

Both dichotomous and multiple-choice questions are difficult to construct, but scoring the items is relatively simple. A file of items may be built up over a period of time so that the same ones don't need to be used on each content test. Each time an item is used, the *item difficulty* may be determined by calculating the percentage of respondents who answered it correctly. If the items in a content test cover a number of behavioural objectives, the respondents should be scored on each objective separately to ascertain whether or not additional instruction is required.

Short-answer content-test items consist of statements or questions that are responded to by a word, number, or a phrase. Recall memory is used in answering short-answer questions whereas recognition memory is involved in dichotomous or multiple-choice items. The short-answer items should have only one correct response which is brief and definite. Don't use statements directly out of a text or other source, and don't construct the statement so that the meaning is lost. Try to place the blank near the end of the statement, and avoid giving clues as to the correct response.

An *essay* content-test item requires the learner to compose a response ranging from one sentence to several pages in length. This type of item, which measures recall memory, permits considerable freedom of expression by the learner and gives him an opportunity to arrange cognitive material in a unique way. Considerable time is required both for answering and scoring essay items, and the scoring tends to be subjective and unreliable. Scoring may be done using either an analytical method, whereby points are allocated to various parts of the response, or a rating method, which sorts the responses into categories based on the answer as a whole.

Types of content-test items:
1. *Dichotomous answer*
2. *Multiple choice*
3. *Short answer*
4. *Essay*

Attitude Scales

There are several types of scales designed to measure learning in the affective domain, but the simplest to construct is known as the Likert type. A statement is presented and the respondent chooses the one response that most accurately represents the direction and intensity of his attitude from a list of three to seven alternate choices. For example, to the statement, "Every part-time instructor should receive training in the principles of adult learning and instruction before he begins teaching," the respondent would check one of the following five responses: 'strongly disagree', 'disagree', 'neutral', 'agree', or 'strongly agree'. An attitude scale usually consists of five to twenty such statements.

Numerical values are assigned to the responses for each statement in order to calculate an attitude score. A statement that was favourable towards the attitude object would be scored 5 points if the respondent strongly agreed and 1 point if he strongly disagreed. That scoring would be reversed if the statement were unfavourable towards the attitude object; 'strongly disagree' would receive 5 points and 'strongly agree' would be scored 1 point. A total attitude-scale score is calculated by adding the scores received on all items in the scale.

Changes in the affective domain can only be determined accurately if before-and-after measurements are taken. The same attitude scale should therefore be administered to the learners both prior to and at the conclusion of instruction. Many attitude scales are available in published articles and books, but most of them deal with psychological or social characteristics such as alienation, dogmatism, power, political attitudes, and so forth. Responses to attitude scales that have been published, as well as those developed for specific purposes by the instructor, are easy to fake, so the instructor should look for additional indicators of attitudes in the behaviour of the learners. In many cases, direct questioning of the course participants by the instructor will yield useful information about learner attitudes towards various aspects of a course.

Rating Scales

The construction of absolute rating scales to evaluate learning in the psychomotor domain involves a sequence of six steps.

1. Define the behavioural objectives as clearly as possible.
2. Determine the traits or factors that determine success or failure in reaching the behavioural objective.
3. Define the critical traits or factors clearly.
4. Determine approximately five degrees of success for each factor.
5. If the factors differ in importance, weight them by assigning higher values to the more important and lower values to the less important factors.
6. Select the best possible form for the rating scale. The most commonly used forms include checklists, numerical scales, and descriptive scales.

Since ratings of psychomotor learning are based on an instructor's judgement and opinion, they are subject to several kinds of error. The *error of central tendency* means that the ratings are grouped close to the average instead of being spread over a wide range. The rating scale is useless if it is applied in that way since it does not reflect the differences in performance that usually exist. The *error of standards* occurs when some instructors under-rate or over-rate everyone compared to the average of all instructor ratings. In that case, the ratings will show differences between instructors rather than differences among learner performances or products. The *error of halo* is found when the ratings made by the instructor are influenced by his general impression of the adult student. To avoid the three common errors in the application of rating scales, the instructor should consider only the specific performance or product being observed in as objective a manner as possible, and should attempt to apply each element of the rating scale as accurately as he can.

> *Common errors in rating:*
> 1. *Error of central tendency*
> 2. *Error of standards*
> 3. *Error of halo*

A CONCLUDING NOTE

Continuous and thorough evaluation is the element that is most frequently lacking in adult-education courses. A systematic programme of evaluation can provide considerable useful information to both the instructor and the learner in order to improve the learning and instructional process. Restricting evaluation to content tests or measures of participant satisfaction overlooks some of the most important sources of information. The instructor should continually look for new and better ways of finding out how much his adult students are learning from the instruction he gives. Instruction can then be adjusted to bring about the maximum amount of learning possible in the limited amount of time that the adult student can commit to an educational activity.

CHAPTER FIVE POST-ASSESSMENT

When you have read chapter five, complete the post-assessment shown below. Indicate whether each statement is true or false and show the degree of confidence in your answer.

Correctness of Statement	Degree of Confidence
T The statement is true.	1 I guessed at the answer.
F The statement is false.	2 My answer may be correct.
	3 I'm confident that my answer is correct.

1. The results of evaluation should not be used in revising objectives. T F 1 2 3
2. An attitude scale measures learner behaviour under natural conditions. T F 1 2 3
3. The first component of an instructional model is pre-assessment of the learners. T F 1 2 3
4. The most useful way to evaluate adult education is by measuring changes in behaviour resulting from the educational activity. T F 1 2 3
5. Evaluation does not indicate whether or not the instruction provided was successful in helping the learners to achieve the behavioural objectives. T F 1 2 3
6. A post-test is used to determine the status of the learners in relation to the objectives of the course. T F 1 2 3
7. The items used in norm-referenced tests must discriminate among learners so that they can be ranked. T F 1 2 3
8. Formative evaluation is used at the end of an educational programme to establish its over-all suitability. T F 1 2 3
9. Evaluating learner performance under natural conditions is referred to as reactive measurement. T F 1 2 3
10. Test items used to measure recognition memory are easy to score but hard to construct. T F 1 2 3

The correct answers are given on the next page.

ANSWERS

1. F; 2. F; 3. F; 4. T; 5. F; 6. T; 7. T; 8. F; 9. F; 10. T

If you answered less than 8 items correctly, re-read chapter five carefully and try to apply the material to your own situation.

FOR FURTHER STUDY

1. Byrn, Darcie, Editor. *Evaluation in Extension.* Topeka, Kansas: H.M. Ives and Sons, 1962. (paperback)

2. DuBois, Philip H. and G. Douglas Mayo, Editors. *Research Strategies for Evaluating Training.* Chicago: Rand McNally, 1970. (paperback)

3. Mager, Robert F. *Developing Attitudes Toward Learning.* Palo Alto, California: Fearon Publishers, 1968. (paperback)

bibliography

CHAPTER ONE—ADULT LEARNING

Bass, Bernard M. and James A. Vaughan. *Training in Industry: The Management of Learning.* Belmont, California: Wadsworth Publishing Company, 1966.

Gagné, Robert M. *The Conditions of Learning.* New York: Holt, Rinehart and Winston, 1970.

Hill, Winfred F. *Learning: A Survey of Psychological Interpretations.* San Francisco: Chandler Publishing, 1963.

Hunter, I.M.L. *Memory.* Harmondsworth: Penguin Books, 1964.

Klausmeier, H.J. and W. Goodwin. *Learning and Human Abilities.* New York: Harper and Row, 1966.

Lorge, Irving *et al. Adult Learning.* Washington, D.C.: Adult Education Association of the U.S.A., 1965.

Mednick, Sarnoff A. *Learning.* Englewood Cliffs, New Jersey: Prentice-Hall, 1964.

Melton, Arthur W. *Categories of Human Learning.* New York: Academic Press, 1964.

Verner, Coolie and Catherine V. Davison. *Psychological Factors in Adult Learning and Instruction.* Tallahassee: Florida State University Adult Education Research Information Processing Center, 1971.

Welford, A.T. *Fundamentals of Skill.* London: Methuen, 1968.

CHAPTER TWO—THE ADULT LEARNER

Bischof, L.J. *Adult Psychology.* Scranton, Pennsylvania: Harper and Row, 1969.

Burns, Robert W., Editor. *Sociological Backgrounds of Adult Education.* Syracuse, New York: Center for the Study of Liberal Education for Adults, 1964.

Dickinson, Gary. "The Learning Abilities of Adults," *Training in Business and Industry*, 6 (1969): 54-55, 74-76.

√ Havighurst, Robert J. and Betty Orr. *Adult Education and Adult Needs*. Chicago: Center for the Study of Liberal Education for Adults, 1956.

Johnstone, John W.C. and Ramon J. Rivera. *Volunteers for Learning: A Study of the Educational Pursuits of American Adults*. Chicago: Aldine Publishing, 1965.

Kidd, J.R. *How Adults Learn*. New York: Association Press, 1959.

Kuhlen, Raymond G., Editor. *Psychological Backgrounds of Adult Education*. Chicago: Center for the Study of Liberal Education for Adults, 1963.

Pressey, Sidney L. and Raymond G. Kuhlen. *Psychological Development Through the Life Span*. New York: Harper and Brothers, 1957.

CHAPTER THREE—COURSE PLANNING

Burns, Richard W. *New Approaches to Behavioral Objectives*. Dubuque, Iowa: William C. Brown, 1972.

√ Gronlund, Norman E. *Stating Behavioral Objectives for Classroom Instruction*. Toronto: Collier-MacMillan Canada, 1970.

Houle, Cyril O. *The Design of Education*. San Francisco: Jossey-Bass, 1972.

Kibler, Robert J., Larry L. Barker and David T. Miles. *Behavioral Objectives and Instruction*. Boston: Allyn and Bacon, 1970.

McMahon, Ernest E. *Needs—of People and Their Communities —and the Adult Educator*. Washington, D.C.: Adult Education Association of the U.S.A., 1970.

√ Mager, Robert F. *Preparing Instructional Objectives*. Palo Alto, California: Fearon Publishers, 1962.

Mager, Robert F. and Kenneth M. Beach. *Developing Vocational Instruction*. Belmont, California: Fearon Publishers, 1967.

Snyder, Robert E. *Decision-Making in the Planning and Imple-*

mentation of Instruction in Adult Basic Education. Tallahassee: Florida State University Adult Education Research Information Processing Center, 1971.

CHAPTER FOUR—INSTRUCTION

Bergevin, Paul E., Dwight Morris and Robert M. Smith. *Adult Education Procedures.* Greenwich, Conn.: Seabury Press, 1963.

Klevins, Chester, Editor. *Materials and Methods in Adult Education.* New York: Klevens Publications, 1972.

Knowles, Malcolm S. *The Modern Practice of Adult Education.* New York: Association Press, 1970.

Leypoldt, Martha M. *40 Ways to Teach in Groups.* Valley Forge: Judson Press, 1967.

Miller, Harry L. *Teaching and Learning in Adult Education.* New York: Macmillan, 1964.

Rogers, Jennifer. *Adults Learning.* Harmondsworth: Penguin Books, 1971.

Schmuck, Richard A. and Patricia A. Schmuck. *Group Processes in the Classroom.* Dubuque, Iowa: William C. Brown, 1971.

Stephens, Michael D. and Gordon W. Roderick. *Teaching Techniques in Adult Education.* Newton Abbot, England: David and Charles, 1971.

Verner, Coolie and Alan Booth. *Adult Education.* New York: Center for Applied Research in Education, 1964.

CHAPTER FIVE—EVALUATION

Bloom, B.S., T.J. Hastings and G.F. Adams. *Handbook on Formative and Summative Evaluation of Student Learning.* Toronto: McGraw-Hill, 1971.

Byrn, Darcie, Editor. *Evaluation in Extension.* Topeka, Kansas: H.M. Ives and Sons, 1962.

Dubois, Philip H. and G. Douglas Mayo, Editors. *Research Strategies for Evaluating Training.* Chicago: Rand McNally, 1970.

Gronlund, Norman E. *Constructing Achievement Tests.* Englewood Cliffs, New Jersey: Prentice-Hall, 1968.

Isaac, Stephen. *Handbook in Research and Evaluation for Education and the Behavioral Sciences.* San Diego: Robert Knapp, 1971.

Knox, Alan B. *Program Evaluation in Adult Basic Education.* Tallahassee: Florida State University Adult Education Research Information Processing Center, 1971.

Miller, Harry L. and Christine H. McGuire. *Evaluating Liberal Adult Education.* Chicago: Center for the Study of Liberal Education for Adults, 1961.

Steele, S.M. *Cost-Benefit Analysis and the Adult Educator: A Literature Review.* Syracuse, New York: E.R.I.C. Clearinghouse on Adult Education, 1971.

Webb, Eugene J. *et al. Unobtrusive Measures.* Chicago: Rand McNally, 1966.

Weiss, Carol H. *Evaluating Action Programs.* Boston: Allyn and Bacon, 1972.